The American
Association
of
Architectural
Bibliographers,
PAPERS, VII

The American Association

Sir Nikolaus Pevsner

# of Architectural Bibliographers

PAPERS, Volume VII, 1970

Edited by William B. O'Neal

Published for
The American Association of
Architectural Bibliographers

The University Press of Virginia
Charlottesville

Contents

Foreword

Gᴀᴏᴡɪɴɢ up into an architectural historian in Germany in the early 1920's was an experience entirely different from that which one would have undergone in England or France. Banister Fletcher's *A History of Architecture on the Comparative Method,* that students' common or garden tool, which had for the first time appeared on the market in 1896 in about 330 pages and was by 1954 (sixteenth edition) grown to well over 1,000 pages, was unknown. So were François Auguste Choisy and Julien Guadet, whose names I heard for the first time when supervising Reyner Banham for his Ph.D. thesis.

Instead the mentors, the exemplars in my case were these. First, Wilhelm Pinder, who held the chair of the history of art at Leipzig, the town where I was born and brought up, and who was a brilliant lecturer, with resources of dazzling ideas and comparisons, and a scholar who thought and felt in terms of *Zeitgeist* and national or regional styles. I learned from him that the history of architecture must not be a pursuit apart from the history of art (as it mostly was in England), and also that presentation matters.

Heinrich Wölfflin was a matter of course. I read him while still at school, for I knew that history of art would be my profession. Here also art and architecture were one and the same, and formulation was taken seriously. Moreover, the conception that the history of art is the history of what and how the eye sees was easily absorbed and had something very tempting.

But my peculiar Leipzig initiation was more than I knew for a long time due to Pinder's predecessor August Schmarsow, still far too little known in Anglo-American circles. He was undoubtedly a powerful source of inspiration for Pinder's treatment of architecture. Schmarsow (1853–1936) in his turn, when he wrote his first and decisive books in the mid-nineties, was inspired by Robert Vischer, the son of the aesthetician Friedrich Theodor Vischer. Friedrich Theodor (1807–87) in his four-volume *System der Aesthetik* had a part on architecture (Pt. III, Sec. II, installment I, *Die Baukunst*, 1852), and this and other parts of the *System* contained ideas made use of by Robert, more strictly an art historian, in his *Über das optische Formgefühl* (1873). The operative idea of this latter book is the "involuntary act of transferring our feelings" into works of art, in short what we now call empathy; Vischer Senior had written: "The vertical raises us, the horizontal widens us, the curved line moves more vividly than the straight line," and this implies "an unconscious transfer of . . . our body . . . into the forms of the object" (*Kritische Gänge*, new ser., installment IV, p. 145). To apply these ideas to architecture was Schmarsow's innovation. Architecture to him is the art of space. This distinguishes it from the other arts, and space is experienced by moving in it, i.e., by the empathic feeling of height, length, and breadth by the human body. Schmarsow's operative books are *Der Wert der drei Dimensionen im menschlichen Raumgebilde* (1893), *Das Wesen der architektonischen Schöpfung* (1894), and *Barock und Rokoko* (1897). The last especially was of the greatest value to me as a historian, not an aesthetician, more than Wölfflin's earlier *Renaissance und Barock* of 1888, and so I began to concentrate on the Baroque. However, in spite of this illustrious pedigree, my thesis on the Baroque architecture of Leipzig was purely a matter of the history of forms, even of motifs. What irks me particularly now is that no consideration was given at all to the peculiar, indeed unique, function of the high merchants' houses. They contained shops and flats and were regularly cleared of domestic tenants for the Leipzig fairs, in order to become exhibition premises to show and sell from samples of merchandise.

No social history then for me in 1923–24, nor much *Geistesgeschichte,* although next to Pinder it was Max Dvořák who impressed me most, with his comprehensive and learned papers on painting of the fourteenth century in Bohemia (1902), his *Rätsel der Brüder van Eyck* (1904), his *Idealismus und Naturalismus in der gotischen Skulptur und Malerei* (1918), and especially his *Kunstgeschichte als Geistesgeschichte,* essays collected in 1924 and including "Greco und der Manierismus."

Of the early development of the Warburg school at Hamburg I noticed little or nothing. After all what Aby Warburg and what F. Saxl wrote was essentially concerned with the iconology of paintings, and this applied also to Erwin Panofsky (*Dürers Kunsttheorie,* 1915; *Idea,* 1924), although valuable papers on architecture were well within the grasp of that remarkable man as well. But there was no iconology of architecture in Warburg circles, nor in those years anywhere else. The operative publications were Richard Krautheimer's of 1942 and Günter Bandmann's *Architektur als Bedeutungsträger* (1951). The former was wholly convincing; the latter and its predecessors, Hans Sedlmayr's *Die Entstehung der Kathedrale* (1950), E. Baldwin Smith's *The Dome* (1950), and A. Stange's *Image of Heaven* (1950), could only be accepted with certain reservations. It is very tempting to present the significance of this or that motif without going to the trouble of attempting to add proof from contemporary sources. This applies for instance to much of Sedlmayr's chapter on the cathedral as the image of heaven. Another example is the lecture I heard by a German friend, who shall remain nameless, interpreting the red alternating with cream stone blocks on the portal of the Emperor Frederick II's Castel del Monte as meaning the imperial purple. My reaction was that, without positive proof, I would only be ready to concur if proof could at least be given that the red stone was specially brought to Apulia from a long distance. If it was local, enjoyment of the duality of color, as at St. Michael in Hildesheim, as at Vézelay, is quite enough. So much for this most recent enrichment of the modes of interpretation of architecture.

My own interpretation began to veer toward social history about 1930. What had happened was that I had turned from Baroque architecture to Mannerist and Baroque painting (Mannerism, thanks to Dvořák and also Pinder's lectures, just then began to absorb some scholars' interest and passion) and found it wanting in power of conviction. When my volume of the *Handbuch der Kunstwissenschaft* was finished in 1928 and I started teaching at Göttingen University, I began to feel the need for an art less rhetorical and more responsible. Three results came from this growing conviction. One was a book called *Academies of Art, Past and Present,* a treatment of art history (not architectural history) as social history; the second was some papers on community ideals among nineteenth-century artists, especially William Morris and C. R. Ashbee; the third a course of about thirty-six lectures at Göttingen on the building types created or reconsidered by nineteenth-century architects. Here was not only an endeavor toward elucidation of the most neglected century of architecture but also a turn from forms per se to functions and the forms, especially of plan, they created.

The book on academies came out finally in England, but the whole preparation for the Göttingen lectures and for my Morrisology was burned, when an incendiary bomb hit the tithe barn in which my papers had been stored. At first the loss was not felt so much, for starting afresh in England meant many new problems, scholarly as well as human. In what ways could a historian of art of German upbringing and mentality be useful in England? What, especially in architectural history, which I more and more specialized in, was lacking? There would no doubt have been a number of answers. Mine were two. When, on a recommendation given by J. M. Richards to Allen Lane, Penguin Books asked me in 1941 to write a paperback history of European architecture (first edition 1942), I tried to make space its focal point—a very belated tribute to the Schmarsow-Pinder past—but to stress social history as well without neglecting history of style. A tall order, and one that failed in various places to varying degrees.

Even more as a response to the feeling of need were the volumes of The Buildings of England series. Their pattern is Georg Dehio's *Handbuch der deutschen Kunstdenkmäler*, initially done by Dehio in 1905–12 in five volumes for the whole of Germany, since expanded into a larger number of volumes. England had nothing of the kind. I suggested it to publishers in 1938–39 but found no promising reception. I intended to go beyond Dehio in two ways: length and autopsy. Instead of five volumes for the whole country there should be one for each English county, and every building—exceptions excepted—should be seen by me and described and analyzed on the spot. Finally after the war, in 1949 to be precise, Penguin Books accepted my scheme, and this has determined my work ever since.

The bibliography that follows—which seems to me to take far too seriously the writings, often casual, of one man—shows that my serious scholarly work has gone thin since The Buildings of England series started. Still, looking back over not just twenty but nearly forty-five years, although I know that I have nowhere propelled my subject—like the Warburg circle and like Ernst Gombrich—I hope to have recognized some needs and provisionally fulfilled them.

NIKOLAUS PEVSNER

London, 1969

SIR NIKOLAUS PEVSNER:
A BIBLIOGRAPHY
Compiled by John R. Barr

Introduction

A Select Bibliography of the Publications of Nikolaus Pevsner" appeared in *Concerning Architecture: Essays on Architectural Writers and Writing Presented to Nikolaus Pevsner,* published in 1968 by Allen Lane, The Penguin Press. It included all his books and major scholarly essays and a selection of his other articles and reviews.

In the bibliography that follows I have listed almost all the writings by Sir Nikolaus published up to the end of 1969 that have come into my hands and a wide selection of reviews of his works by others. Within each section of the bibliography, except that of book reviews by Sir Nikolaus, the works are arranged by year, and within each year alphabetically by title; the arrangement of The Buildings of England series, however, is entirely chronological. All translations, new editions, extracts, reprints, and reviews of a work are listed in one place under the original or first edition.

Where it has not been possible to give exact references to some early newspaper articles and reviews, they have been recorded in a collective entry only. Book reviews by Sir Nikolaus published anonymously in the *Times Literary Supplement* are given only up to the end of 1965.

Pagination is given as printed in each book or journal; the number of plates is stated only where the plates are numbered separately from the main pagination.

In a selection made by Sir Nikolaus, twenty-eight of his articles and essays were reissued in 1968 in *Studies in Art, Architecture, and Design*. Two volumes were published by Thames and Hudson, and texts originally in foreign languages were translated there into English. All these are marked with an asterisk in this bibliography.

Sir Nikolaus's work as an editor is outside the scope of this record of his work as an author. He has been an editor of the *Architectural Review* since 1941. He edited for the Architectural Press *Bombed Churches as War Memorials*, 1945. He edited the King Penguin series for Penguin Books; he is editor of their forty-six-volume *Pelican History of Art*, and has been since its inception. Of this series thirty volumes have so far been published.

I am very grateful to Sir Nikolaus not only for his permission to expand the Festschrift bibliography but also for his help and advice, especially in making available his own file of offprints and clippings.

JOHN R. BARR

London, 1969

Chronology and Honors

Sir Nikolaus Pevsner, C.B.E., F.B.A., M.A. Cantab., M.A. Oxon., Ph.D. Leipzig, F.S.A., Hon. F.R.I.B.A., Hon. A.R.C.A., Hon. F.N.Z.I.A., Hon. Academician Accademia di Belle Arti di Venezia, Hon. Member American Academy of Arts and Sciences, Hon. Member Göttinger Gesellschaft der Wissenschaften.

1902	Born January 30 in Leipzig
1924	Ph.D., Leipzig University
1924–28	Assistant Keeper, Dresden Art Gallery
1928–33	Lecturer in the History of Art and Architecture, University of Göttingen
1933	Settled in London
1944–59	Lecturer in the History of Art, Birkbeck College, University of London
1947—	Member of the editorial board, *Architectural Review*
1949	Hon. Associate of the Royal College of Art
1949–55	Slade Professor of Fine Art, University of Cambridge
1950–55	Fellow of St. John's College, Cambridge
1950	Fellow of the Society of Antiquaries

1953	Commander of the Order of the British Empire
1955	BBC Reith Lecturer
1955—	Council member, William Morris Society
1959–67	Professor of the History of Art, Birkbeck College, University of London
1959—	Member, National Advisory Council for Art Education
1961—	Member, National Council for Diplomas in Art and Design
1962—	Member, Arts Panel, British Council
1963—	Chairman of the Victorian Society
1963	Awarded Howland Memorial Prize, Yale University
1963–68	Commissioner, Royal Commission on Historic Monuments
1965	Fellow of the British Academy
1966—	Member, Royal Fine Art Commission
	Member, Historic Buildings Council
1966	Awarded Alice Davis Hitchcock Medallion by the Society of Architectural Historians of Great Britain
	Hon. D.Litt., University of Leicester
1967	Awarded Royal Institute of British Architects Royal Gold Medal
	Hon. Fellow, Royal Institute of British Architects
	Hon. Fellow, St. John's College, Cambridge
	Hon. D.Univ., University of York
	Hon. D.Litt., University of Leeds
1968–69	Slade Professor of Fine Art, University of Oxford
1968	Hon. LL.D., University of Oxford
1969	Knighted for services to art history
	Vice-president, William Morris Society
	Hon. D.Litt., University of East Anglia
	Grand Cross of Merit, Federal Republic of Germany

Writings by Sir Nikolaus Pevsner

BOOKS AND MONOGRAPHS

1928

With Otto Grautoff. *Barockmalerei in den romanischen Ländern.* Teil 1. *Die italienische Malerei vom Ende der Renaissance bis zum ausgehenden Rokoko.* By Dr. Nikolaus Pevsner. 214 pp. Teil 2. *Die Malerei im Barockzeitalter in Frankreich und Spanien.* By Dr. Otto Grautoff. 333 pp. Wildpark-Potsdam: Akademische Verlagsgesellschaft Athenaion, 1928. 20 pls. Illus. (Handbuch der Kunstwissenschaft.)

> REVIEWS:
> *Bücherwelt,* Jan. 28, 1931, p. 375. (Gottwald.)
> *Burlington Magazine,* 58 (April, 1931), 202–3. (Of Teil 1 only.)

Leipziger Barock. Die Baukunst der Barockzeit in Leipzig. Dresden: Wolfgang Jess, 1928. 208 pp. 102 pls. Plans.

> REVIEWS:
> *Die Denkmalpflege: Zeitschrift für Denkmalpflege und Heimatschutz,* 1930, p. 296. (Wolfgang Herrmann.)
> *Das schöne Sachsen,* Jan. 1934, p. 432.
> *Zeitschrift für bildende Kunst,* 65 (July, 1931), "Kunstchronik" pp. 37–38. (Otto Holtze.)

1936

Pioneers of the Modern Movement from William Morris to Walter Gropius.
London: Faber and Faber, 1936. 240 pp. Illus. American edition: New
York: Frederick A. Stokes Co., 1936; reprinted 1937.
> REVIEWS:
> *Architect and Building News,* Dec. 11, 1936, p. 318.
> *Architects' Journal,* 84 (Nov. 12, 1936), 673.
> *Architectural Association Journal,* 53 (Aug., 1937), 131.
> *Architectural Forum,* 67 (Nov., 1937), suppl. p. 30.
> *Architectural Review,* 80 (Nov., 1936), 218–21. Illus.
>   (P. Morton Shand.)
> *Art and Industry,* 21 (Nov., 1936), 202–5. (John Gloag.)
> *Artist,* 2 (Dec., 1936), xii.
> *Burlington Magazine,* 70 (Jan., 1937), 49. (G. Price-Jones.)
> *Journal of the Royal Institute of British Architects,* 3rd ser.,
>   44 (March, 1937), 456–57. (R. McGrath.)
> *Listener,* Oct. 14, 1936, suppl. p. xviii. (Herbert Read.)
> *Manchester Guardian,* Oct. 9, 1936. (Eric Newton.)
> *Metron,* no. 41–42 (May–Aug., 1951), pp. 101–5. (Enrico
>   Tedeschi. "La storia dell'architettura moderna da Pevsner
>   a Zevi.")
> *Parnassus,* 11 (April, 1939), 29. (A. Philip McMahon.)
> *Times Literary Supplement,* Dec. 5, 1936, p. 1010.

Pioneers of Modern Design from William Morris to Walter Gropius.
2nd ed. [of *Pioneers of the Modern Movement*]. New York:
Museum of Modern Art, 1949. 151 pp. Illus. Reprinted 1957.
> REVIEWS:
> *Architectural Review,* 108 (Nov., 1950), 326.
> *Journal of the Royal Institute of British Architects,* 3rd ser.,
>   57 (June, 1950), 321.

Revised and partly rewritten edition. Harmondsworth: Penguin
Books, 1960. 253 pp. Illus. (Pelican Books, A497.)
> REVIEW:
> *Architectural Review,* 129 (Jan., 1961), 6.

[Corrected edition with a bibliography of new literature.] Harmondsworth: Penguin Books, 1964. 255 pp. Illus. Reprinted 1966,
1968.

REVIEWS:
Listener, June 8, 1967, pp. 743–71. Illus. (Richard Sheppard.)
New York Times, Jan. 17, 1965, p. 50. (Wayne Andrews.)

TRANSLATIONS

I pionieri del movimento moderno da William Morris a Walter Gropius. Tr. by Giuliana Baracco. Milan: Rosa e Ballo, 1945. viii, 130 pp. 8 pls.
REVIEW:
Metron, no. 6 (Jan., 1946), pp. 71–73. (E. T.)

I pionieri dell'architettura moderna. Tr. by Enrica Labò. Bologna: Edizioni Calderini, 1963. xiv, 215 pp. (Città nuova, 2.)

Wegbereiter moderner Formgebung von Morris bis Gropius. Tr. by Elisabeth Knauth. Hamburg: Rowohlt, 1957. 142 pp. Pls. Bibliog. (Rowohlts deutsche Enzyklopädie, 33.)
REVIEWS:
Baukunst und Werkform (Nuremberg), 1958, no. 10.
Christliche Kunstblätter (Linz), 1958, pt. 2.
Die Innenarchitektur (Essen), Sept., 1958.
Mosaik (Studentenzeitung, Munich), 1959, no. 7.
Der Tagesspiegel (Berlin), Feb. 1, 1959.
Die Weltwoche, Aug. 29, 1958.

Modan dezain no tenkai [The Development of Modern Design]. Tr. by Hirozō Shiraishi. Tokyo: Misuzu Shobō, 1957. 167 pp. 33 pls.

Pioneros del diseño moderno. Tr. by Odilia Suárez and Emma Gregoros. Buenos Aires: Ediciones Infinito, 1960. 236 pp. Illus.

Os pioneiros do desenho moderno. Tr. by João Paulo Monteiro. Lisbon: Editora Ulisseia, [1964]. 190 pp. Illus. (Colecção Livros Pelicano, AM8.)

Pionirji modernega oblikovanja. Tr. by Helena Menaše. Ljubljana: Mladinska knjiga, 1966. 165 pp. 24 pls.

1937

An Enquiry into Industrial Art in England. Cambridge: University Press, 1937. xi, 234 pp. 24 pls.
REVIEWS:
Apollo, 26 (April, 1938), 213.

Architectural Forum, 67 (Nov., 1937), suppl. p. 116.

Architectural Review, 82 (Aug., 1937), 73–74. Illus. (John Gloag.)

Art and Industry, 23 (July, 1937), 23–25. Illus. Comments by manufacturers, *ibid.* (Sept., 1937), pp. 112–14.

Arts and Decoration, 47 (Oct., 1937), 47. (J. Vassos.)

Commonweal, 26 (Aug. 27, 1937), 426.

Connoisseur, 102 (July, 1938), 48. (R. W. S.)

Economic Journal, 47 (Dec., 1937), 729–32. (Josiah Wedgwood.)

Journal of the Royal Institute of British Architects, 3rd ser., 44 (July, 1937), 891. (John Gloag.)

Manchester Guardian, June 15, 1937. (Eric Newton.)

New Statesman, Sept. 4, 1937, p. 350. (L. Andrews.)

Parthenon, 11 (Sept., 1937), 419.

Scrutiny, 6 (Dec., 1937), 316–25. (J. M. Harding.)

Spectator, June 11, 1937, p. 1102.

Springfield Republican, July 23, 1937.

Times Literary Supplement, July 17, 1937, p. 522.

1938

With Sacheverell Sitwell. *German Baroque Sculpture.* London: Duckworth, 1938. 48 pls. Bibliog. With 48 photographs by Anthony Ayscough and descriptive notes by Nikolaus Pevsner, pp. 49–84.

> REVIEWS:
> *Apollo,* 28 (July, 1938), 36.
> *Architectural Review,* 84 (Sept., 1938), 127–28. (Osbert Lancaster.)

1940

Academies of Art, Past and Present. Cambridge: University Press, 1940. xiv, 323 pp. Pls. Bibliog. American edition: New York: Macmillan, 1940.

> REVIEWS:
> *Architectural Review,* 88 (July, 1940), 30. (Percy Horton.)
> *Art Bulletin,* 23 (June, 1941), 184–85. (Robert J. Goldwater.)
> *Burlington Magazine,* 78 (April, 1941), 134. (Herbert Read.)

Connoisseur, 106 (July, 1940), 41.

De Gids, 104 (1940, dl. 4), 188–89.

Journal of the Royal Society of Arts, 89 (June 27, 1941), 507–8. (Tancred Borenius.)

Magazine of Art, 33 (Aug., 1940), 484–85. (Gertrude R. Benson.)

Parnassus, 12 (Nov., 1940), 25. (H. W. Janson.)

Studio, 120 (Oct., 1940), 140. (R. D.)

Sunday Times, May 12, 1940, p. 4. (Desmond MacCarthy.)

Times Literary Supplement, May 4, 1940, p. 216.

1942

An Outline of European Architecture. Harmondsworth; New York: Penguin Books, 1942. 159 pp. 32 pls. Plans. Bibliog. (Pelican Books, A109.)

REVIEWS:

Architects' Journal, Aug. 26, 1943, pp. 153–54. (Herbert Read.)

Architectural Review, 94 (July, 1943), 26. (Geoffrey Webb.)

Journal of the Royal Institute of British Architects, 3rd ser., 50 (Aug., 1943), 239. (R. H. S.)

Studio, 126 (Sept., 1943), 96. (Oswald P. Milne.)

Times Literary Supplement, Nov. 6, 1943, p. 537.

Tribune, July 23, 1943, p. 18.

Revised and enlarged edition. Harmondsworth: Penguin Books, 1945. 237 pp. 48 pls.

REVIEWS:

Architectural Review, 99 (Feb., 1946), 64.

Sunday Times, Nov. 18, 1945.

New and enlarged edition. London: John Murray, 1948. xxi, 238 pp. Pls. Illus. Plans. Bibliog. First American edition: New York: Charles Scribner's Sons, 1948.

REVIEWS:

Country Life, Aug. 13, 1948, p. 343. (A. S. O.)

Journal of Aesthetics and Art Criticism, 8 (March, 1950), 200–201. (Paul Zucker.)

Journal of the Royal Institute of British Architects, 3rd ser., 55 (Sept., 1948), 515.

Manchester Guardian, July 16, 1948. (J. W.)

Nation, Dec. 4, 1948, p. 644. (Albert Guerard.)

New Yorker, Jan. 8, 1949. (Lewis Mumford. "Skyline.")
Spectator, July 23, 1948, p. 118. (Lionel Brett.)

Second revised [i.e. third] edition. Harmondsworth: Penguin Books, 1951. 301 pp. 64 pls. Illus. Plans. Bibliog. Additions on French Gothic, French seventeenth century, and Italian Mannerism.

REVIEWS:

Journal of the Royal Institute of British Architects, 3rd ser., 58 (June, 1951), 331.
Tablet, May 12, 1951, pp. 380–81.
Times Literary Supplement, April 27, 1951, p. 266.
Tribune, May 18, 1951.

Fourth edition, revised and enlarged. Harmondsworth: Penguin Books, 1953. 317 pp. 64 pls. Illus. Plans. Bibliog. Reprinted 1954.

Fifth edition, revised and enlarged. Harmondsworth: Penguin Books, 1957. 328 pp. 64 pls. Illus. Plans. Bibliog. Reprinted 1958, 1959, 1961. Additions on Early Christian, Byzantine, and French eighteenth century.

REVIEW:

Architects' Journal, Dec. 12, 1957, p. 872. ("Astragal.")

Sixth jubilee edition. Harmondsworth: Penguin Books, 1960. 740 pp. Illus. Plans. Bibliog. Reprinted 1961. Most of the 609 illustrations were from photographs collected by the Prestel Verlag for the German edition of 1957, and the section on German Baroque (pp. 414–74) was translated from that edition. The new last chapter deals with developments from 1914 onwards.

REVIEWS:

Apollo, 73 (Jan., 1961), 25. (E. D. Mills.)
Architectural Review, 129 (Jan., 1961), 6.
Art Bulletin, 43 (March, 1961), 74–75. (J. S. Ackerman.)
Burlington Magazine, 103 (Nov., 1961), 469–70. (Clifford Musgrave.)
Connoisseur, 147 (June, 1961), 288. (J. L.-M.)
Journal of the Society of Architectural Historians, 20 (Oct., 1961), 150.
New Statesman, Jan. 20, 1961, p. 100. (John Summerson.)
Observer, Dec. 11, 1960. (R. Furneaux Jordan.)
Scientific American, July, 1961, p. 180.
Sunday Standard (Bombay), Dec. 10, 1961.
Times Literary Supplement, Dec. 9, 1960, p. 792.

Seventh edition. Harmondsworth: Penguin Books, 1963. 496 pp. Illus. Plans. Bibliog. Reprinted with revised bibliog., 1968.

REVIEWS:
Journal of the Royal Institute of British Architects, 3rd ser.,
70 (Aug., 1963), 332.
New York Times, Sept. 18, 1963, p. 25. (Ada L. Huxtable.)
TRANSLATIONS
Geschiedenis van de bouwkunst in Europa. Tr. by E. Kossmann.
Rotterdam: Ad. Donker, 1949. xiv. 360 pp. Illus. Later edition:
1960. xiv. 273 pp. Illus. (Donker-pockets, 32.) Reprinted 1962,
1965.
REVIEW:
Literair Maandblad, 12 (Feb., 1950).

Yōroppa kenchiku josetsu [An Introduction to European Architec-
ture]. Tr. by Bunji Kobayashi. Tokyo: Shōkokusha Publishing
Co., 1953. xiv, 292 pp. Pls. Plans. Bibliog. Reprinted 1963.

Esquema de la arquitectura europea. Spanish translation revised and
enlarged by René Taylor. Revised by Emilio Orozco Díaz. Buenos
Aires: Ediciones Infinito, 1957. 351 pp. Pls. Plans. Bibliog.
(Biblioteca de arquitectura, 2.) Second edition: Additions tr. by
Francisco Bullrich. 1968. 503 pp.
REVIEW:
Revista de ideas esteticas, 20 (Jan.–March, 1962), 3–29.
(Alonso R. Gutiérrez de Ceballos. "La arquitectura del
manierismo.")

Europäische Architektur von den Anfängen bis zur Gegenwart. Tr.
by Kurt Windels. Munich: Prestel Verlag, 1957, 740 pp. Illus.
Plans. Bibliog. Later edition, 1963. 547 pp. (Studienausgabe.)
The section on German baroque was new, and most of the hun-
dreds of photographs were especially collected for this edition.

Storia dell'architettura europea. Preface by Mario Labò. Translation
by Enrica Labò supplemented from the German edition of 1957.
Bari: Laterza, 1959. xi, 407 pp. Pls. Plans. Bibliog. (Biblioteca
di cultura moderna, 535.) Second edition, 1963. 418 pp. Later
edition, 1966. 427 pp. (Universale Laterza, 42.)
REVIEWS:
Casabella, no. 232 (Oct., 1959), pp. 29–31. Illus. (Leonardo
Benevolo.)
Cultura Moderna, July, 1959, pp. 1–4. (Leonardo Benevolo.)
Zodiac, no. 5 (1960), pp. 198–99. (G. V. "L'architecture
en trois histoires: Hitchcock, Sartoris, Pevsner.")

Storia dell'architettura europea. Translation by Enrica Labò supplemented from the German edition of 1963. Milan: Il Saggia-
tore, 1966. 735 pp.

REVIEWS:

Le Arte, 65 (Dec., 1966).

Domus, no. 477, Feb., 1967. (Agnoldomenico Pica.)

La Fiere Letteraria, Jan. 12, 1967. (Lorenza Trucchi.)

Il Popolo, Jan. 10, 1967.

Il Tempo, Dec. 14, 1966. (Mario Praz.)

Génie de l'architecture européenne. Tr. by Renée Plouin. Paris: Hachette; Tallandier, 1965. 430 pp. Illus. Plans. Bibliog.

Perspectiva da arquitectura europeia. Tr. by Ernesto de Sousa. Lisbon: Ulisseia, [1965]. 420 pp. Pls. (Livros pelicano, AM15.)

Oris evropske architekture. Tr. by Helena Menaše. Ljubljana: Državna založba slovenije, 1966. 446 pp. Illus. Plans. Bibliog. (Kultura in zgodovina.)

Euroopan arkkitehtuurin historia. Tr. by Raija Mattila and Pekka Suhonen. Helsinki: Otava, 1968. 476 pp. Illus.

Iniciació a l'arquitectura. Tr. by Joan Antoni Roig i Fransitorra. Catalan ed. revised by Jaume Freixa. Barcelona: Edicions 62, 1969. 286 pp. Preface by Oriol Bohigas. (Biblioteca bàsica de cultura contemporània, 22.)

1945

The Leaves of Southwell. Photographs by F. L. Attenborough. London and New York: Penguin Books, 1945. 71 pp. 32 pls. Illus. Plan. (King Penguin Books, K17.)

REVIEWS:

Architectural Forum, 84 (June, 1946), 142–46. Illus. (J. M. F.)

Architectural Record, 99 (March, 1946), 28.

Architectural Review, 99 (June, 1946), 184. (Joan Evans.)

Burlington Magazine, 88 (April, 1946), 103–4. (B. R.)

1946

Visual Pleasures from Everyday Things: An Attempt to Establish Criteria by Which the Aesthetic Qualities of Design Can Be Judged. London: B. T. Batsford, 1946. 19 pp. Illus. (Council for Visual Education Booklet, no. 4.)

1950

*Charles R. Mackintosh.** Tr. by Cornelia Tamborini. Milan: Il Balcone, 1950. 151 pp. Pls. Illus. Bibliog. (Architetti del movimento moderno, 8.)
> REVIEW:
> *Architectural Review*, 110 (Sept., 1951), 203–4. (G. C. Argan.)

*Matthew Digby Wyatt, The First Cambridge Slade Professor of Fine Art.** Cambridge: University Press, 1950. 44 pp. 6 pls. Bibliog. An inaugural lecture. Abridged version: *Listener*, Nov. 10, 1949, pp. 807–9. Illus.
> REVIEWS:
> *Architectural Review*, 112 (Sept., 1952), 195. (C. L. V. Meeks.)
> *Art Bulletin*, 34 (Dec., 1952), 325. (Robert W. Duemling.)
> *Times Literary Supplement*, Dec. 8, 1950, p. 782.

1951

*High Victorian Design: A Study of the Exhibits of 1851.** London: Architectural Press, 1951. 162 pp. Illus.
> REVIEWS:
> *Architectural Record*, 110 (Dec., 1951), 44.
> *Architectural Review*, 113 (Feb., 1953), 123. (C. H. Gibbs-Smith.)
> *Burlington Magazine*, 94 (Aug., 1952), 240–41. (Charles Mitchell.)
> *Cambridge Review*, March 1, 1952, pp. 346–48. (Geoffrey Best.)
> *College Art Journal*, 11, no. 4, (1952), 301–2. (G. H. Huntley.)
> *Journal of the Royal Institute of British Architects*, 3rd ser., 59 (Nov., 1951), 26.
> *Manchester Guardian*, Aug. 3, 1951. (Lawrence Haward.)
> *Progressive Architecture*, 33 (Feb., 1952), 150.
> *Spectator*, Oct. 12, 1951, p. 488. (C. E. V.)
> *Times Literary Supplement*, Aug. 10, 1951, p. 496.

* Reprinted in *Studies in Art, Architecture, and Design*, 1968.

1954

Cánones de la crítica. Tr. by Raul Gonzalez Capdevila. Buenos Aires:
   Facultad de Arquitectura y Urbanismo, Universidad de Buenos Aires;
   Ministerio de Educación, 1954. A translation of the article on the
   Coventry Cathedral competition, *Architectural Review*, Jan., 1951.

1956

The Englishness of English Art. London: Architectural Press, 1956. 208
   pp. Illus. Plans. An expanded and annotated version of the Reith
   Lectures broadcast in October and November 1955. American edition:
   New York: Praeger, 1956. Originally published in *The Listener*, Oct.
   20–Dec. 1, 1955. Introduction published in a pamphlet, *The Reith
   Lectures, 1955: The Englishness of English Art.* London: BBC, 1955.
   REVIEWS:
   Apollo, 63 (June, 1956), 236–37. Illus. (Helen Lowenthal.)
   Architectural Review, 120 (Sept., 1956), 193. (Herbert
      Read.)
   Arts, 31 (May, 1957), 35–36. (Vernon Young.)
   Daily Telegraph, April 27, 1956.
   Journal of Aesthetics, 15 (June, 1957), 492–93. (Paul
      Zucker.)
   Journal of the Royal Institute of British Architects, 3rd ser.,
      64 (April, 1957), 237. (W. A. Eden.)
   Manchester Guardian, April 20, 1956. (Mario Praz.)
   New Statesman, April 14, 1956, p. 382. (John Berger.)
   Observer, April 8, 1956. (R. Furneaux Jordan.)
   Spectator, July 6, 1956, p. 36. (Basil Taylor.)
   Sunday Times, April 8, 1956.
   Times Literary Supplement, May 25, 1956, p. 312.

   Later edition. Harmondsworth: Penguin Books, 1964. 229 pp. Illus.
      Plans. (Peregrine Books, Y35.)
      REVIEWS:
      Canadian Art, 21 (Nov.–Dec., 1964), 382. (T. A. Heinrich.)
      Comment, May 23, 1964. (Jack Dunman.)

1958

Christopher Wren, 1632–1723. Tr. into Italian by Enrica Labò. Milan: Electa, 1958. 64 pl. Plans. Bibliog. (Astra-Arengarium. Collana di monografie d'arte. Serie architetti, 45.)

> REVIEW:
> *Journal of the Royal Institute of British Architects,* 3rd ser., 65 (Sept., 1958), 394.

American edition: *Christopher Wren, 1632–1723.* New York: Universe Books, 1960. 64 pls. Plans. Bibliog. (Universe Books architecture series.)

> REVIEW:
> *Architectural Record,* 129 (April, 1961), 57.

With Michael Meier. *Grünewald.* London: Thames and Hudson, 1958. 44 pp. 117 + 26 pls. "An Introduction to Grünewald's Art," pp. 9–19. Bibliog. American edition: New York: Harry N. Abrams, 1958.

> REVIEWS:
> *Burlington Magazine,* 101 (July–Aug., 1959), 295–96. (L. D. Ettlinger.)
> *Christian Science Monitor,* July 3, 1958. (Dorothy Adlow.)
> *Illustrated London News,* March 29, 1958, p. 518. (Frank Davis.)
> *Observer,* April 20, 1958. (Geoffrey Grigson.)
> *Spectator,* April 11, 1958, p. 464. (Alan Bowness.)
> *Studio,* 156 (July, 1958), 32. (Michael Ayrton.)
> *Times Literary Supplement,* April 18, 1958, p. 204.

1961

The Planning of the Elizabethan Country House. London: Birkbeck College, 1961. 24 pp. 4 pls. Plans. An inaugural lecture delivered at Birkbeck College, May 23, 1960.

> REVIEW:
> *Times Literary Supplement,* July 14, 1961, p. 438.

With Jean Cassou and Emile Langui. *Les sources du vingtième siècle.* Paris: Editions des Deux-Mondes, 1961. 363 pp. Pls. Illus. (L'art et la culture.) "L'architecture et les arts appliqués, par Nikolaus Pevsner," pp. 229–60.

Belgian edition: Brussels: Editions de la Connaissance, 1961. (Collection "Le Conseil de l'Europe," 2.) Originally published as the Catalogue of the Council of Europe exhibition in Paris, 1960.

TRANSLATIONS

Durchbruch zum 20. Jahrhundert: Kunst und Kultur der Jahrhundertwende. Tr. by Eleonore Seitz [and others]. Munich: Georg D. W. Callwey, 1962.

Gateway to the Twentieth Century: Art and Culture in a Changing World. New York: McGraw-Hill, 1962.

> REVIEW:
>
> *Art Journal,* 22 (1962–63), 274–76. (Alan M. Fern.)

Le origini dell'arte moderna. Tr. by Enrica Labò [and others]. Milan: Electa, 1962.

The Sources of Modern Art. Tr. by Katherine M. Delavenay and H. Leigh Farnell. London: Thames and Hudson, 1962.

> REVIEWS:
>
> *Arts Review,* May 5, 1962 (Pierre Rouve.)
> *Daily Telegraph,* April 19, 1962. (H. D. Ziman.)
> *Listener,* June 22, 1962, p. 1127. (Herbert Read.)
> *Manchester Guardian,* Dec. 14, 1962.
> *New Statesman,* Sept. 14, 1962, p. 332. (Andrew Forge.)
> *Observer,* June 10, 1962. (Alan Bowness.)
> *Studies: An Irish Quarterly Review,* Autumn, 1962, pp. 432–38. (John C. Kelly.)
> *Studio,* 166 (Nov., 1963), 215. (J. P. Hodin.)
> *Sunday Telegraph,* April 29, 1962.

Reprinted as *The Sources of Modern Architecture and Design.* London: Thames and Hudson, 1968. 216 pp. Illus. Plans. Bibliog. (World Library of Art.)

> REVIEWS:
>
> *Architectural Design,* 38 (July, 1968), 299.
> *Design,* Oct., 1968, p. 78. (Gillian Naylor.)
> *Hampstead and Highgate Express,* June 7, 1968. (Christopher Gotch.)
> *Industrial Architecture,* July, 1968, p. 337.
> *Jewish Chronicle* (Property Supplement), June 28, 1968. (Misha Black.)
> *New Society,* June 6, 1968. (Reyner Banham.)
> *Sunday Telegraph,* Nov. 3, 1968. (Michael Hanson.)
> *Times,* July 13, 1968. (Tony Richardson.)
> *Times Educational Supplement,* June 28, 1968.

Times Literary Supplement, Feb. 20, 1969, p. 190.
Yorkshire Post, Nov. 9, 1968.

Génesis del siglo XX. Barcelona: Salvat, 1963.

1963

The Choir of Lincoln Cathedral: An Interpretation. London; New York: Oxford University Press, 1963. 15 pp. Pls. Plans. Charlton Lectures on Art delivered at King's College in the University of Durham, Newcastle upon Tyne.

> REVIEWS:
> *Architectural Review*, 134 (July, 1963), 6.
> *Times Literary Supplement*, June 28, 1963, p. 482.

1966

Fünfhundert Jahre Künstlerausbildung. William Morris. Zwei Vorträge; Bauhaus-Archiv, Darmstadt, Staatliche Kunstakademie, Düsseldorf. Darmstadt: Roether-Druck, 1966. 24 pp. Illus.

With John Fleming and Hugh Honour. *The Penguin Dictionary of Architecture.* Harmondsworth: Penguin Books, 1966. 248 pp. Illus. Plans. (Pelican Reference Books, R13.) Nikolaus Pevsner wrote the entries on mediaeval, nineteenth-century, and twentieth-century architecture, also the European and American national entries, and most of the stylistic entries.

> REVIEWS:
> *Architectural Review*, 139 (May, 1966), 325.
> *Times Literary Supplement*, Feb. 24, 1966, p. 149.

1968

Studies in Art, Architecture, and Design. 2 vols. Vol. 1: *From Mannerism to Romanticism.* Vol. 2: *Victorian and After.* London: Thames and Hudson, 1968. Illus. Bibliog. Collected articles, papers, and essays. (Indicated by * in this bibliography.)

> REVIEWS:
> *Architects' Journal*, Dec. 11, 1968. (Reyner Banham.)
> *Architectural Review*, 146 (Oct., 1969), 322–23. (Francis Haskell.)

Design, Feb., 1969, p. 74. (Christopher Cornford.)
Illustrated London News, Jan. 4, 1969. (Andrew Causey.)
Journal of the Royal Institute of British Architects, 3rd ser.,
    75 (Dec., 1968), 552. (Nicholas Taylor.)
New Society, Dec. 19, 1968. (John Berger.)
Observer, Jan. 26, 1969. (Robin Middleton.)
Spectator, Nov. 22, 1968. (Stephen Gardiner.)
Studio, 177 (March, 1969), 145–46. (Joseph Masheck.)
Sunday Telegraph, Nov. 3, 1968. (Michael Hanson.)
Sunday Times, Oct. 27, 1968. (Nicholas Taylor. "The
    Compleat Perambulator.")
Times, Nov. 30, 1968. (David Piper.)
Yorkshire Post, Nov. 9, 1968.
The Year's Art. 1968–69. London: Hutchinson, 1969, pp.
    123–24. (Cyril Barrett. "Art Books.")
American edition. New York: Walker and Co., 1968.
    REVIEW:
    New York Times, Aug. 10, 1969. (Rackstraw Downes.)

1969

*Ruskin and Viollet-le-Duc: Englishness and Frenchness in the Appreciation
    of Gothic Architecture.* London: Thames and Hudson, 1969 [1970].
    48 pp. Illus. Walter Neurath Memorial Lecture.

THE BUILDINGS OF ENGLAND SERIES

1951

Cornwall. Harmondsworth: Penguin Books, 1951. 251 pp. 64 pls. Map.
    (Buildings of England, BE1.)
            REVIEWS:
            Architect and Building News, Aug. 16, 1951.
            Architects' Journal, Aug. 9, 1951, pp. 153, 155. ("Astragal.")
            Architectural Record, 110 (Sept., 1951), 30.
            Architectural Review, 112 (Dec., 1952), 399. (Ernest
                Savage.)

Art News and Review, Sept. 8, 1951. (David Waring.)
Burlington Magazine, 94 (July, 1952), 212. (Margaret Whinney.)
Connoisseur, 128 (Dec., 1951), 196. (L. G. G. R.)
Cornish Times, July 27, 1951.
Daily Mirror, July 27, 1951.
History Today, 1 (Nov., 1951), 75. (Geoffrey Grigson.)
Journal of the Royal Institute of British Architects, 3rd ser., 59 (Feb., 1952), 141. (T. S. Attlee.)
Listener, Oct. 4, 1951, p. 562. (J. M. Richards.)
Municipal Journal, March 28, 1952, p. 669.
New Statesman, Sept. 15, 1951, pp. 285–86. (John Summerson.)
Observer, July 29, 1951. (Geoffrey Grigson.)
Punch, Nov. 7, 1951. (J. P. T.)
Tablet, Nov. 17, 1951, p. 359.
Times Literary Supplement, July 20, 1951, p. 453.
Western Evening Herald, July 26, 1951.

Nottinghamshire. Harmondsworth: Penguin Books, 1951. 248 pp. 64 pls. Map. (Buildings of England, BE2.)

REVIEWS:

Architect and Building News, Aug. 16, 1951.
Architects' Journal, Aug. 9, 1951, pp. 153, 155. ("Astragal.")
Architectural Design, 21 (Sept., 1951), 280. (B. R.)
Architectural Review, 112 (Dec., 1952), 399. (Ernest Savage.)
Art News and Review, Sept. 8, 1951. (David Waring.)
Burlington Magazine, 94 (July, 1952), 212. (Margaret Whinney.)
Connoisseur, 128 (Dec., 1951), 196. (L. G. G. R.)
Journal of the Royal Institute of British Architects, 3rd ser., 59 (April, 1952), 222–23. (C. St.C. Oakes.)
Listener, Oct. 4, 1951, p. 562. (J. M. Richards.)
Municipal Journal, March 28, 1952, p. 669.
New Statesman, Sept. 15, 1951, pp. 285–86. (John Summerson.)
Nottingham Evening Post, Sept. 6, 1951.
Nottingham Guardian, Sept. 11, 1951.
Nottingham Journal, July 27, 1951.
Observer, July 29, 1951. (Geoffrey Grigson.)
Punch, Nov. 7, 1951. (J. P. T.)
Tablet, Nov. 17, 1951, p. 359.

Times Literary Supplement, July 20, 1951, p. 453.
Worksop Guardian, Feb. 28, 1951.

Middlesex. Harmondsworth: Penguin Books, 1951. 204 pp. 64 pls. Map.
(Buildings of England, BE3.)

REVIEWS:

Architectural Review, 113 (May, 1953), 331. (N. G. Brett
James.)
Listener, Nov. 1, 1951, p. 757. (W. F. Grimes.)
Manchester Guardian, June 26, 1953. (James Bone.)
Middlesex County Times, Oct. 20, 1951.
Municipal Journal, March 28, 1952, p. 669.
Punch, Nov. 7, 1951. (J. T. P.)
Surveyor, Oct. 19, 1951.

1952

North Devon. Harmondsworth: Penguin Books, 1952. 200 pp. 48 pls. Map.
(Buildings of England, BE4.)

REVIEWS:

Devon and Exeter Gazette, June 27, 1952.
Journal of the Royal Institute of British Architects, 3rd ser.,
60 (March, 1953), 198–99. (H. V. M. R.)
North Devon Journal–Herald, June 26, 1952.
Time and Tide, Sept. 27, 1952.
Times Literary Supplement, July 11, 1952, p. 459.
Western Morning News, June 30, 1952.

South Devon. Harmondsworth: Penguin Books, 1952. 351 pp. 80 pls. Map.
Plan. (Buildings of England, BE5.)

REVIEWS:

Architect and Building News, Sept. 18, 1952, p. 356.
Dartmouth Chronicle, July 25, 1952.
Journal of the Royal Institute of British Architects, 3rd ser.,
60 (March, 1953), 198–99. (H. V. M. R.)
South Devon Journal, July 16, 1952.
South Devon Times, July 18, 1952.
Time and Tide, Sept. 27, 1952.
Times Literary Supplement, Sept. 19, 1952, p. 618.
Western Evening Herald, July 26, 1952.
Western Morning News, May 8, 1959.

London, except the Cities of London and Westminster. Harmondsworth:
Penguin Books, 1952. 496 pp. 64 pls. Map. (Buildings of England,
BE6.) Reprinted 1969.

REVIEWS:
Architects' Journal, Aug. 7, 1952, p. 155. ("Astragal.")
Ibid., Jan. 15, 1953, p. 110. (Reyner Banham.)
Architects' Journal, Aug. 7, 1952, p. 155. ("Astragal.")
  Reddaway.)
Art News and Review, July 12, 1952.
Builder, Sept. 26, 1952, p. 425.
Building, Sept., 1952, p. 321, 323.
Burlington Magazine, 95 (July, 1953), 254. (M. D. W.)
Daily Worker, Aug. 14, 1952.
Jewish Chronicle, Sept. 5, 1952.
John o' London's Weekly, Aug. 8, 1952. (William Gaunt.)
Journal of the Institute of Town Planning, Feb., 1953, p. 69.
Journal of the Royal Institute of British Architects, 3rd ser.,
  60 (March, 1953), 198–99. (H. V. M. R.)
Listener, Oct. 23, 1952, pp. 689–91.
Muemlek Vedelem (Budapest), 1963, pp. 122–23. (László
  Gerö.)
New Hungarian Quarterly, 3 (July–Sept., 1962), 36–37.
  (Ivan Boldizsár.)
Official Architecture, 115 (Aug., 1952), 375.
Spectator, July 11, 1952, p. 76.
Surveyor, July 19, 1952, p. xv.
Times Literary Supplement, Aug. 29, 1952, p. 558.

1953

Hertfordshire. London: Penguin Books, 1953. 313 pp. 64 pls. Map. (Buildings of England, BE7.)

REVIEWS:
Architectural Review, 115 (March, 1954), 206. (Ian Nairn.)
Journal of the Royal Institute of British Architects, 3rd ser.,
  60 (Sept., 1953), 459. (H. V. M. R.)

Derbyshire. London: Penguin Books, 1953. 282 pp. 64 pls. Map. (Buildings
of England, BE8.)

REVIEWS:
Architects' Journal, Aug. 6, 1953, p. 155. ("Astragal.")
Architectural Review, 115 (March, 1954), 206. (Ian Nairn.)

Derby Evening Telegraph, Aug. 20, 1953.
Derbyshire Advertiser, June 19, 1953.
Derbyshire Countryside, Summer, 1953.
Journal of the Royal Institute of British Architects, 3rd ser.,
    60 (Sept. 1953), 459. (H. V. M. R.)

County Durham. London: Penguin Books, 1953. 279 pp. 64 pls. Map.
(Buildings of England, BE9.) Entries on Roman aniqtuities by Prof.
Ian A. Richmond.

REVIEWS:

Architectural Association Journal, 69 (Nov., 1953), 116.
    (Mary Nattrass.)
Architectural Review, 115 (March, 1954), 206. (Ian Nairn.)
    Letter by C. Gotch, *ibid.*, 116 (July, 1954), 2.
Burlington Magazine, 96 (Jan., 1954), 26. (Bruce Allsopp.)
    Letter by F. John and reply by Nikolaus Pevsner, *ibid.*,
    (July, 1954), p. 214.
Journal of the Royal Institute of British Architects, 3rd ser.,
    60 (Sept., 1953), 459. (H. V. M. R.)
Listener, Aug. 13, 1953, p. 271.
New Durham (Magazine of the students of Durham Colleges),
    June, 1953, pp. 28–29.
Newcastle Evening Chronicle, May 29, 1953; Sept. 25, 1953.
Northern Echo, May 22, 1953.
Shields Gazette, May 22, 1953.
Shipley Times and Express, Sept. 1, 1953.
Times Literary Supplement, July 3, 1953, p. 426.

1954

Cambridgeshire. Harmondsworth: Penguin Books, 1954. 453 pp. 72 pls.
Map. Plans. (Buildings of England, BE10.)

REVIEWS:

Architectural Review, 117 (Feb., 1955), 131. (J. McQ.)
Burlington Magazine, 98 (July, 1956), 247. (Kenneth Har-
    rison.)
Cambridge Review, June 4, 1955, p. 605. (M. H. Bräude.)
Journal of the Royal Institute of British Architects, 3rd ser.,
    62 (June, 1955), 344. (Peter Bicknell.)
Kunstchronik, 8 (June, 1955), 172–73. (Ernst Gall.)
Listener, Feb. 10, 1955, p. 257.
Oxford Mail, Dec. 16, 1954.

    Tablet, June 11, 1955. (Richard Butcher.)
    Times Educational Supplement, Dec. 24, 1954.
    Times Literary Supplement, May 6, 1955, p. 242.

Essex. London: Penguin Books, 1954. 440 pp. 64 pls. Illus. Map. Plan.
(Buildings of England, BE11.) 2nd ed. Revised by Enid Radcliffe. 1965.
482 pp. 64 pls.

    REVIEWS:
    Builder, Aug. 27, 1954.
    Burlington Magazine, 96 (Oct., 1954). (G. Montagu Ben-
        ton.)
    Colchester and County Notes, July 16, 1954.
    Journal of the Royal Institute of British Architects, 3rd ser.,
        62 (Dec., 1954), 74. (H. V. M. R.)
    *Leytonstone Express and Independent and Essex County Rec-
        ord*, July 20, 1958.
    Stratford Express, Aug. 13, 1954.
    Times Literary Supplement, Aug. 6, 1954, p. 503.
    West Essex Gazette, July 2, 1954.

1957

London. I. *The Cities of London and Westminster*. Harmondsworth:
Penguin Books, 1957. 631 pp. 96 pls. Map. Plans. (Buildings of England, BE12.)

    REVIEWS:
    Architect and Surveyor, July–Aug., 1958, p. 88.
    Architects' Journal, May 2, 1957, p. 656. ("Astragal.")
    Burlington Magazine, 99 (Nov., 1957), 390. (Margaret
        Whinney.)
    Connoisseur, 143 (April, 1959), 182.
    Evening News, April 20, 1957.
    Evening Standard, April 23, 1957. (Richard Church.)
    Hampstead Express, May 24, 1957.
    Indicator, May 11, 1957.
    Jewish Chronicle, May 10, 1957.
    Journal of the Royal Institute of British Architects, 3rd ser.,
        64 (Oct., 1957), 508. (H. V. M. R.)
    Listener, July 25, 1957, pp. 141–42.
    Manchester Guardian, June 14, 1957. (Eric de Maré.)
    New Hungarian Quarterly, 3 (July–Sept., 1962), 36–37.
        (Ivan Boldizsár.)

New Statesman, June 15, 1957, pp. 776–77. (G. W. Stonier.)
Observer, April 28, 1957. (Geoffrey Grigson.)
Revue d'histoire ecclésiastique, 53, pt. 1 (1958), 320.
Spectator, May 24, 1957, pp. 683–84. (John Betjeman.)
Sunday Times, May 19, 1957. (Raymond Mortimer.)
Tablet, June 1, 1957.
Time and Tide, May 11, 1957. (Alec Clifton-Taylor.)
Times, May 24, 1957.
Times Educational Supplement, May 24, 1957, p. 723.
Times Literary Supplement, May 17, 1957, p. 310.

Second edition 1962. 696 pp. 96 pls. Maps. Plans. This edition contains a complete index of all streets and buildings.

REVIEWS:
Architect and Building News, March 27, 1963, p. 479, (D. W.)
Muemlek Vedelem (Budapest), 1963, pp. 122–23. (László Gerö.)
New Statesman, Sept. 28, 1962, p. 427. (Reyner Banham.)

Northumberland. Harmondsworth: Penguin Books, 1957. 362 pp. 64 pls. Map. Plan. (Buildings of England, BE12 [i.e., BE15].) With notes on the Roman antiquities by Ian A. Richmond.

REVIEWS:
Burlington Magazine, 100 (Feb., 1958), 68. (Nicholas Ridley.)
Daily Telegraph, Jan. 3, 1958. (John Betjeman.)
Journal of the Royal Institute of British Architects, 3rd ser., 65 (April, 1958), 204. (H. V. M. R.)
Northumberland Gazette, Nov. 22, 1957.
Times Educational Supplement, Jan. 10, 1958, p. 24.
Times Literary Supplement, Jan. 10, 1958, p. 21.

1958

North Somerset and Bristol. Harmondsworth: Penguin Books, 1958. 510 pp. 72 pls. Map. Plan. (Buildings of England, BE13.)

REVIEWS:
Architect and Building News, Nov. 19, 1958, p. 690. (Bryan Little.)
Architects' Journal, May 1, 1958. ("Astragal.")
Bristol Evening World, April 3, 1958.
Daily Telegraph, June 6, 1958. (John Betjeman.)

Journal of the Royal Institute of British Architects, 3rd ser.,
  65 (Oct., 1958), 432. (H. V. M. R.)
Listener, Jan. 15, 1959, p. 139. (W. G. Hoskins.)
Time and Tide, June 21, 1958, pp. 777–78. (Alec Clifton-
  Taylor.)
Times Educational Supplement, April 11, 1958, p. 562.
Times Literary Supplement, April 25, 1958, p. 228.

South and West Somerset. Harmondsworth: Penguin Books, 1958. 394 pp.
  56 pls. Map. (Buildings of England, BE14.)
  REVIEWS:
    Architect and Building News, Nov. 19, 1958, p. 690. (Bryan
      Little.)
    Daily Telegraph, June 6, 1958. (John Betjeman.)
    Journal of the Royal Institute of British Architects, 3rd ser.,
      65 (Oct., 1958), 432. (H. V. M. R.)
    Time and Tide, June 21, 1958, pp. 777–78. (Alec Clifton-
      Taylor.)
    Times Literary Supplement, July 25, 1958, p. 419.

Shropshire. Harmondsworth: Penguin Books, 1958. 368 pp. 64 pls. Map.
  (Buildings of England, BE16.)
  REVIEWS:
    Architect and Building News, Dec. 17, 1958, p. 820.
    Architects' Journal, Dec. 4, 1958, p. 805. ("Astragal.")
    Architectural Association Journal, 74 (Feb., 1959), 214.
      (Peter Matthews.)
    Birmingham Post, Dec. 23, 1958.
    Burlington Magazine, 102 (Jan., 1960), 43. (James Lees-
      Milne.)
    County Express (Stourbridge), Jan. 13, 1959.
    Daily Worker, Sept. 24, 1959.
    Journal of the Royal Institute of British Architects, 3rd ser.,
      66 (July, 1959), 328. (H. V. M. R.)
    Listener, Jan. 15, 1959, p. 139. (W. G. Hoskins.)
    Municipal Review, Aug., 1959.
    Times Educational Supplement, Jan. 23, 1959.
    Times Literary Supplement, March 13, 1959, p. 147.

1959

Yorkshire: The West Riding. Harmondsworth: Penguin Books, 1959. 603
  pp. 72 pls. Map. Plan. (Buildings of England, BE17.) 2nd ed. Revised
  by Enid Radcliffe. 1967. 652 pp.

REVIEWS:
Architect and Building News, Sept. 23, 1959, pp. 219–20.
(D. W.)
Architects' Journal, Feb. 18, 1960, p. 284.
Architectural Review, 128 (Oct., 1960), 323. (Ian Nairn.)
Bradford Telegraph and Argus, June 18, 1959.
Dalesman, July, 1959, pp. 247–48.
Huddersfield Weekly Courier and Guardian, May 30, 1959.
Huddersfield Weekly Examiner, Aug. 15, 1959.
Journal of the Royal Institute of British Achitects, 3rd ser.,
67 (Dec., 1959), 64. (H. V. M. R.)
Keighley News, May 30, 1959.
Municipal Review, Nov., 1959, p. 662.
South Yorkshire Times, May 23, 1959.
Times Literary Supplement, Sept. 4, 1959, p. 504.
Yorkshire Post, May 29, 1959.

1960

Leicestershire and Rutland. Harmondsworth: Penguin Books, 1960. 373 pp.
64 pls. Map. (Buildings of England, BE18.)
REVIEWS:
Architect and Building News, Aug. 10, 1960.
Architectural Review, 128 (Oct., 1960), 323. (Ian Nairn.)
Birmingham Post, March 15, 1960.
Daily Telegraph, April 8, 1960.
Journal of the Royal Institute of British Architects, 3rd ser.,
68 (April, 1961), 244. (J. H.)
Leicester Mercury, Feb. 26, 1960.
Listener, May 12, 1960, p. 854. (W. G. Hoskins.)
Times Literary Supplement, July 1, 1960, p. 421.
Buckinghamshire. Harmondsworth: Penguin Books, 1960. 340 pp. 64 pls.
Map. Plan. (Buildings of England, BE19.)
REVIEWS:
Architect and Building News, Dec. 14, 1960, p. 778. (D. W.)
Architectural Review, 128 (Oct., 1960), 323. (Ian Nairn.)
Birmingham Post, April 4, 1961.
Bucks Free Press, Oct. 1, 1960.
Builder, 199 (Oct. 7, 1960), 661. (M. S. B.)
Journal of the Royal Institute of British Architects, 3rd ser.,
68 (April, 1961), 244. (J. H.)

Listener, Nov. 10, 1960, p. 856. (W. G. Hoskins.)
Municipal Review, Jan., 1961, p. 55.
Records of Buckinghamshire, 16 (1960), 370–71. (E. C. R.)
Times Educational Supplement, Nov. 18, 1960, p. 666.
Times Literary Supplement, Sept. 30, 1960, p. 631.

1961

Suffolk. Harmondsworth: Penguin Books, 1961. 516 pp. 64 pls. (Buildings
of England, BE20.)
REVIEWS:
Beccles and Bungay Journal, Aug. 17, 1962.
Eastern Daily Press, March 10, 1961.
Journal (Bungay), April 28, 1961.
Listener, April 20, 1961, p. 708. (W. G. Hoskins.)
Manchester Guardian, March 13, 1961. (Geoffrey Moor-
house.)
Observer, April 23, 1961. (Angus Wilson.)
Spectator, March 24, 1961, p. 425. (Kenneth J. Robinson.)
Times Literary Supplement, March 24, 1961, p. 188.
Northamptonshire. Harmondsworth: Penguin Books, 1961. 510 pp. 64 pls.
Map. Plan. (Buildings of England, BE22.)
REVIEWS:
Architectural Forum, May, 1962, p. 185. (W. McQ.)
Northampton Chronicle and Echo, Aug. 31, 1961.
Northamptonshire Antiquarian Society Reports and Papers,
63 (1960–61), 34–36.
Northamptonshire Evening Telegraph, Aug. 31, 1961.
Times Educational Supplement, Sept. 30, 1961, p. 363.
Times Literary Supplement, Oct. 6, 1961, p. 665. Letter by
Nikolaus Pevsner, *ibid.*, Oct. 13, 1961, p. 683.

1962

With Ian Nairn. *Surrey.* Harmondsworth: Penguin Books, 1962. 501 pp.
64 pls. Map. (Buildings of England, BE21.)
REVIEWS:
Daily Telegraph, Sept. 21, 1962.
Manchester Guardian, June 15, 1962. (Geoffrey Moorhouse.)
Observer, April 29, 1962. (Alec Clifton-Taylor.)

Sunday Telegraph, April 22, 1962. (Fello Atkinson.)
Tablet, June 9, 1962.
Times Literary Supplement, May 11, 1962, p. 337.

North-East Norfolk and Norwich. Harmondsworth: Penguin Books, 1962.
   390 pp. 64 pls. Map. Plan. (Buildings of England, BE23.)

North-West and South Norfolk. Harmondsworth: Penguin Books, 1962.
   438 pp. 64 pls. Map. (Buildings of England, BE24.)
   REVIEWS OF BOTH VOLUMES:
   Architectural Forum, 44 (Oct., 1962), 179. (W. McQ.)
   Connoisseur, 151 (Dec., 1962), 218–19. (Alec Clifton-
      Taylor.)
   Journal of the Royal Institute of British Architects, 3rd ser.,
      70 (Sept., 1963), 378. (S. Rowland Peirce.)
   New Statesman, Sept. 28, 1962, p. 427. (Reyner Banham.)
   Norwich Eastern Daily Press, June 29, 1962. (R. W. Ketton-
      Cremer.)
   Tablet, Aug. 4, 1962, p. 736.
   Times Literary Supplement, Nov. 2, 1962, p. 838.

1963

Herefordshire. London: Penguin Books, 1963. 364 pp. 64 pls. Map. Plan.
   (Buildings of England, BE25.)
   REVIEWS:
   Antiquaries' Journal, 44, pt. 1 (1964), 79. (F. C. Morgan.)
   Connoisseur, 155 (Jan., 1964), 50. (Alec Clifton-Taylor.)
   Manchester Guardian, May 10, 1963. (Geoffrey Moorhouse.)
   Times Literary Supplement, June 7, 1964, p. 403.

Wiltshire. Harmondsworth: Penguin Books, 1963. 578 pp. 64 pls. Map.
   Plans. (Buildings of England, BE26.)
   REVIEWS:
   Connoisseur, 155 (Jan., 1964), 50. (Alec Clifton-Taylor.)
   Observer, Aug. 11, 1963. (Geoffrey Grigson.)
   Times Literary Supplement, Nov. 1, 1963, p. 880.
   Wiltshire Times and News, July 5, 1963.

1964

With John Harris: *Lincolnshire.* Harmondsworth: Penguin Books, 1964.
   768 pp. 64 pls. Map. Plan. (Buildings of England, BE27.)

REVIEWS:
Architectural Review, 137 (Feb., 1965), 99. (John Piper.)
Connoisseur, 160 (Dec., 1965), 258. (Alec Clifton-Taylor.)
Journal of the Royal Institute of British Architects, 3rd ser.,
     72 (Oct., 1965), 519. (J. C. P.)
New Statesman, July 9, 1965, p. 54. (N. Wollaston.)
Tablet, Dec. 12, 1964. (Tudor Edwards.)
Times Literary Supplement, Oct. 29, 1964, p. 983.

1965

With Ian Nairn: *Sussex*. London: Penguin Books, 1965. 692 pp. 64 pls.
   Maps. (Buildings of England, BE28.) West Sussex by Ian Nairn.
        REVIEWS:
        Architectural Review, 140 (Sept., 1966), 160–61. (Priscilla
             Metcalf.)
        Connoisseur, 163 (Dec., 1966), 266–67. (Alec Clifton-
             Taylor.)
        Daily Telegraph, Aug. 19, 1965.
        Listener, July 15, 1965, p. 97. (Alec Clifton-Taylor.)
        Manchester Guardian, July 16, 1965. (Geoffrey Moorhouse.)
        Spectator, Sept. 3, 1965, p. 296. (A. Robertson.)
        Times, June 24, 1965.
        Times Literary Supplement, Aug. 5, 1965, p. 682.

1966

Yorkshire: The North Riding. Harmondsworth: Penguin Books, 1966. 454
   pp. 64 pls. Map. Plan. (Buildings of England, BE29.)
        REVIEWS:
        Antiquaries' Journal, 47, pt. 1 (1967), 128. (Eric Gee.)
        Architect and Building News, June 22, 1966.
        Architectural Review, 140 (Sept., 1966), 160–61. (Priscilla
             Metcalf.)
        Connoisseur, 163 (Dec., 1966), 266–67. (Alec Clifton-
             Taylor.)
        Manchester Guardian, March 31, 1966. (Geoffrey Moor-
             house.)
        Northern Daily Mail (West Hartlepool), March 10, 1966.
        Times Literary Supplement, April 21, 1966, p. 350.

Berkshire. Harmondsworth: Penguin Books, 1966. 355 pp. 64 pls. Map.
  Plans. (Buildings of England, BE30.)
> REVIEWS:
> *Antiquaries' Journal,* 47, pt. 2 (1967), 306–7. (F. M. Under-
>   hill.)
> *Architect and Building News,* June 22, 1966.
> *Architectural Review,* 141 (Feb., 1967), 95. (Priscilla Met-
>   calf.)
> *Connoisseur,* 163 (Dec., 1966), 266–67. (Alec Clifton-
>   Taylor.)
> *Times Literary Supplement,* Aug. 18, 1966, p. 741.

With Alexandra Wedgwood. *Warwickshire.* Harmondsworth: Penguin
  Books, 1966. 529 pp. 64 pls. Maps. Plan. (Buildings of England, BE31.)
  Birmingham by Alexandra Wedgwood.
> REVIEWS:
> *Antiquaries' Journal,* 47, pt. 2 (1967), 307. (W. B.
>   Stephens.)
> *Architectural Review,* 141 (Feb., 1967), 95. (Priscilla Met-
>   calf.)
> *Birmingham Evening Mail and Despatch,* July 27, 1966.
> *Connoisseur,* 163 (Dec., 1966), 266–67. (Alec Clifton-
>   Taylor.)
> *Listener,* Jan. 12, 1967, p. 62. (W. G. Hoskins.)
> *Manchester Guardian,* Aug. 18, 1966. (Geoffrey Moorhouse.)
> *Times,* Aug. 11, 1966.
> *Times Literary Supplement,* Aug. 18, 1966, p. 741.

1967

With David Lloyd. *Hampshire and the Isle of Wight.* Harmondsworth:
  Penguin Books, 1967. 832 pp. Pls. Map. Plans. (Buildings of England,
  BE32.) David Lloyd describes Southampton and Portsmouth and the
  towns and villages between and around them.
> REVIEWS:
> *Antiquaries' Journal,* 48, pt. 1 (1968), 129–30. (Jack
>   Blakiston.)
> *Architectural Review,* 143 (April, 1968), 254–55. (Priscilla
>   Metcalf.)
> *Connoisseur,* 167 (Jan., 1968), 50. (A. C.-T.)
> *New Statesman,* June 16, 1967, p. 848. (Osbert Lancaster.)
> *New York Times,* July 8, 1967, p. 27. (E. Fremont-Smith.)

Observer, April 2, 1967. (Ian Nairn.)
Saturday Review, June 24, 1967, p. 28. (T. Bishop.)
Sunday Times, April 30, 1967. (Cyril Connolly.)
Times Literary Supplement, May 25, 1967, p. 432.
Yorkshire Post, Aug. 17, 1968.

Cumberland and Westmoreland. Harmondsworth: Penguin Books, 1967.
339 pp. Pls. Illus. Map. (Buildings of England, BE33.)
REVIEWS:
Architectural Review, 143 (April, 1968), 254–55. (Priscilla
Metcalf.)
Connoisseur, 167 (Jan., 1968), 50.
Times Literary Supplement, Oct. 12, 1967, p. 965.
Yorkshire Evening Press, Aug. 31, 1967.

1968

Bedfordshire, Huntingdon, and Peterborough. Harmondsworth: Penguin
Books, 1968. 414 pp. Pls. Illus. Map. Plans. (Buildings of England,
BE34.) The section on the Soke of Peterborough was first published in
The Buildings of England, BE22, in 1961 as part of *Northamptonshire.*
REVIEWS:
Bedfordshire Magazine, Summer, 1968, pp. 227–28.
Bedfordshire Times, May 24, 1968.
Luton Evening Post, April 25, 1968.

Worcestershire. Harmondsworth: Penguin Books, 1968. 376 pp. Pls. Illus.
Plans. (Buildings of England, BE35.)
REVIEWS:
Stourbridge County Express, Aug. 23, 1968.
Sunday Times, Aug. 18, 1968. (Nicholas Taylor.)
Times Literary Supplement, Oct. 3, 1968, p. 1135.

1969

Lancashire. I. The Industrial and Commercial South. Harmondsworth:
Penguin Books, 1969. 480 pp. Illus. Map. Plan. (Buildings of England,
BE36.)

Lancashire. II. The Rural North. Harmondsworth: Penguin Books, 1969.
306 pp. Illus. Map. (Buildings of England, BE37.)

REVIEW:
Times Literary Supplement, Jan. 22, 1970, p. 72. [Review of
both volumes.]

ARTICLES ON THE BUILDINGS OF ENGLAND SERIES

"English Buildings," *Times Literary Supplement,* July 20, 1951, p. 435.
Leading article.
The Highway (Workers' Educational Association), Jan., 1953, pp. 155–57.
(Helen Lowenthal.)
Journal of the Society of Architectural Historians, 15 (May, 1956), 29.
(Alan Gowans.)
"A Great Interpreter," *Sunday Times,* Feb. 6, 1959. ("Atticus.")
"A Day with the Pevsners," *Manchester Guardian,* April 21, 1960.
"Guiding Principles," *Times Literary Supplement,* Jan. 26, 1967, p. 67.
Leading article.
Sunday Times, April 30, 1967. (Cyril Connolly.)

CONTRIBUTIONS TO BOOKS

1929

"Magnasco, Alessandro; Magnasco, Stefano," *in* Ulrich Thieme and Felix
Becker, eds. *Allgemeines Lexikon der bildenden Künstler.* Leipzig: E. A.
Seeman, 1907–50. Vol. 23 (1929), 560–61.

1946

"The Architecture of Mannerism," *in* Geoffrey Grigson, ed. *The Mint: A
Miscellany of Literature, Art, and Criticism.* London: Routledge, 1946.
pp. 116–37. Plates. Bibliog.
REVIEW:
Sunday Times, May 4, 1947. (Desmond MacCarthy.)

Translation. "La arquitectura del Manierismo," tr. by Marina Waisman, in *Boletín Bibliográfico, Instituto interuniversitario de especialización en historia de la arquitectura* (Córdoba, Argentina), no. 5 (July, 1964), 7–25.

1949

Foreword, *in* Helmut Gernsheim. *Focus on Architecture and Sculpture: An Original Approach to the Photography of Architecture and Sculpture, with a Foreword by Nikolaus Pevsner.* London: Fountain Press, 1949. pp. 9–13.

1951

"A Century of Industrial Design and Designers, 1851–1951," in *Designers in Britain, 1851–1951: A Biennial Review of Graphic and Industrial Design Compiled by the Society of Industrial Artists.* London: The Society, 1951. Vol. 3, pp. 175–82.

1953

"A Note on the Art of the Exeter Carvers," *in* C. J. P. Cave. *Mediaeval Carvings in Exeter Cathedral.* Harmondsworth: Penguin Books, 1953. 64 pls. Illus. Plan. (King Penguin Books, K41.) pp. 25–32.
REVIEW:
Listener, Jan. 31, 1956, p. 152.

1955

Foreword and Postscript, *in* Michael Farr. *Design in British Industry: A Mid-Century Survey.* Cambridge: Cambridge University Press, 1955. Foreword: pp. xxvii–xxviii. Postscript: pp. 310–20.

Introduction, in *The Reith Lectures, 1955: The Englishness of English Art.* London: BBC, 1955. pp. 1–8. The plates in this pamphlet illustrate the Reith Lectures to be broadcast weekly on the Home Service from October 16, 1955, until November 27, 1955.

1956

"Bavarian Rococo—or the Eloquent in Art, by Nikolaus Pevsner, from
a Broadcast on the BBC Third Programme, Nov., 1954," *in* Victoria
and Albert Museum. *Rococo Art from Bavaria.* London: Lund
Humphries, 1956. [4] pp.

Foreword, *in* H. A. N. Brockman. *The Caliph of Fonthill.* London: Werner
Laurie, 1956. pp. xi–xiii.

"Palladio and Europe," in *Venezia e l'Europa.* Venice: Arte Veneta, 1956.
pp. 81–94. Acts of the 18th International Congress of Art History,
Venice, September 12–18, 1955.

1959

"Art Nouveau," in *Encyclopedia of World Art.* Vol. 1. New York, Toronto,
London: McGraw-Hill, 1959. Col. 811–14. Pl. 466–70.

1960

"Architecture and the Applied Arts," in *The Sources of the XXth Century:
The Arts in Europe from 1884 to 1914.* Paris: Musée National d'Art
Moderne, 1960, 1961. pp. 41–55. Pls. Catalogue of the Council of Europe
Exhibition, Paris, Nov. 4, 1960—Jan. 23, 1961.

> French edition. "L'architecture et les arts appliqués," in *Les sources
> du XXe siècle: Les arts en Europe de 1884 à 1914.* Paris, 1960,
> 1961. pp. xli–lvi.

"Art and Architecture," in *New Cambridge Modern History.* Vol. 10, *1830–
70.* Cambridge: University Press, 1960. Ch. 6, pp. 134–55.

"Art and Architecture," *in* Sir William Emrys Williams, ed. *The Reader's
Guide.* Harmondsworth: Penguin Books, 1960. (Pelican Books, A500.)
pp. 45–70. An annotated reading list with an introduction.

1961

Introductions, *in* J. M. Richards, ed. *New Buildings in the Commonwealth.*
London: Architectural Press, 1961. Illus. Pt. 1: The Larger Dominions.

General introduction by Nikolaus Pevsner, pp. 13–16. New Zealand. Introduction by Nikolaus Pevsner, pp. 43–45.

1962

"Art and Architecture," in *New Cambridge Modern History*. Vol. 11, *1870–98*. Cambridge: Cambridge University Press, 1962. Ch. 6, pp. 154–76.

1963

"Victorian Prolegomena," and "Richard Norman Shaw," *in* Peter Ferriday, ed. *Victorian Architecture*. London: Jonathan Cape, 1963. pp. 21–36, 235–46. Pls. Illus.
> REVIEWS:
> *Architectural Review*, 135 (Dec., 1964), 394. (H.-R. Hitchcock.)
> *Progressive Architecture*, 46 (April, 1965), 268. (P. Collins.)

"Visión de la arquitectura en 1963," in *Arquitectura 63*. Barcelona: Publicación de la Escuela Tecnica Superior de Arquitectura de Barcelona, [1963]. pp. 9–12. Illus.
> Translation. "Un allarme de Nikolaus Pevsner: Si ritorna all' architettura di facciata?" *L'architettura*, 9 (Oct., 1963), 482–83.

1964

Foreword, *in* Alan Salvidge. *The Parsonage in England, Its History and Architecture*. London: S.P.C.K., 1964. pp. xiii–xv.

Foreword, *in* Nicholas Taylor. *Cambridge New Architecture: A Guide to the Post-War Buildings*. Cambridge: Published by the Editors at Trinity Hall, 1964. Illus. Plans. Map. pp. 8–9.

Introduction, in *Maxwell Fry*. Eccles, Lancs.: Monks Hall Museum, 1964. Illus. Bibliog. An exhibition catalogue with an introduction by Nikolaus Pevsner.

"Lutyens, Edwin Landseer," in *Encyclopedia of World Art*. Vol. 9. New York, Toronto, London: McGraw-Hill, 1964. Col. 353–54.

1965

"History of the DIA [Design and Industries Association]," * in *DIA Yearbook*, 1965. Illus. pp. 34–52. Fiftieth anniversary issue.

Introduction, *in* Arts Council of Great Britain. *Art Nouveau in Great Britain*. [London], 1965. pp. 2–4. An exhibition catalogue.

"Möglichkeiten und Aspekte des Historismus: Versuch einer Frühgeschichte und Typologie des Historismus," pp. 13–24; "Diskussion unter Leitung von Nikolaus Pevsner," pp. 73–106; "Nachwort," pp. 107–13; "Anhang: Die Wiederkehr des Historismus," pp. 116–17, in *Historismus und bildende Kunst: Vorträge und Diskussion im Oktober 1963 in München und Schloss Anif*. Munich: Prestel Verlag, 1965. (Forschungsunternehmen der Fritz Thyssen Stiftung. Arbeitskreis Kunstgeschichte: Studien zur Kunst des neunzehnten Jahrhunderts, Bd. 1.)

"Morris, William," in *Encyclopedia of World Art*. Vol. 10. New York, Toronto, London: McGraw-Hill, 1965. Col. 323–24.

"Prospect and Retrospect, by the Editor," in *The Pelican History of Art: New and Forthcoming Volumes and Complete List of Series*. Harmondsworth: Penguin Books, [1965]. 1 p. A brochure.

1966

Introduction *in* Ludwig Münz and Gustav Künstler. *Adolf Loos: Pioneer of Modern Architecture* [Der Architekt Adolf Loos]. Tr. by Harold Meek. London: Thames and Hudson, 1966. With an appreciation by Oskar Kokoschka. Introduction, pp. 13–22.

"An Introduction to Modern Architecture," *in* British Broadcasting Corporation. *For Sixth Forms: 4 Modern Buildings*. London, 1966. pp. 12–14. Illus. BBC Television for schools, Summer Term, 1966.

1967

Introduction, *in* Oscar Beyer, ed. *Eric Mendelsohn: Letters of an Architect*. Tr. by Geoffrey Strachan. London, New York, Toronto: Abelard-Schuman, 1967. pp. 13–20.

* Reprinted in *Studies in Art, Architecture, and Design*, 1968.

"Kunst um 1900: Einleitung (des Sektionleiters)," in *Stil und Überlieferung in der Kunst des Abendlandes: Akten des 21. Internationalen Kongresses für Kunstgeschichte in Bonn, 1964*. Berlin, 1967. Bd. 1, pp. 239–40.

"A Master Plan," in *You Live Here: The Story of Hampstead Garden Suburb*. London, 1967. pp. 23–31.

1968

"L'art gothique dans le monde anglo-saxon," in *L'Europe gothique, XIIe-XIVe siècles*. Paris: Musée du Louvre, Pavillon de Flore, 1968. pp. xxxiii–xxxviii. Illus. An exhibition catalogue for the 12th exhibition of the Council of Europe.

Foreword, *in* Alison Smithson and Peter Smithson. *The Euston Arch and the Growth of the London, Midland, and Scottish Railway*. London: Thames and Hudson, 1968. [2] pp.

Foreword, *in* Andor Gomme and David W. Walker. *Architecture of Glasgow*. London: Lund Humphries, 1968. pp. 8–10.

1969

"Introduction: The City and Its Builders," *in* James L. Howgego. *The City of London through Artists' Eyes, with an Introduction by Nikolaus Pevsner*. London: Collins, 1969. pp. 9–11. Illus.

CONTRIBUTIONS TO PERIODICALS

1924

"Regesten zur Leipziger Baukunst der Barockzeit," *Neues Archiv für sächsische Geschichte und Altertumskunde*, 45 (1924), 104–20.

1925

[Articles and reviews of exhibitions in Dresden, etc.], *Dresdner Anzeiger*, 1925:

"Beckmann-Ausstellung," 1925.

"Neue Kunst Fides: Jawlenski-Ausstellung," 1925.

"Ausstellung plastischer Werke von Georg Kolbe, Galerie Arnold," March 20, 1925.

"Ludwig Meidner: Ausstellung in der Kunsthandlung Emil Richter," March 23, 1925.

"El Lissitzky: Kunsthandlung Kühl und Kühn," March 31, 1925.

"Dresdner Kunstausstellungen: Ausstellung japanesischer Farben-holzschnitte," March 31, 1925.

"Sturmausstellung: Neue Kunst Fides," April 5, 1925.

"Gedächtnisausstellung Hans Thoma: Kunstausstellung Emil Rich-ter," April 17, 1925.

"Edmund Möllers Freiheitsdenkmal für Peru," April 29, 1925.

"Galerie Arnold: Hodler, Huf, Kirchner," May 4, 1925.

"Graphisches Kabinett Hugo Erfurth Hofer-Ausstellung," May 7, 1925.

"Max Lehrs zum 70. Geburtstag," June 23, 1925.

"Felixmüller und Böckstiegel Ausstellung bei Hugo Erfurth," July 1, 1925.

"Rheinische Jahrtausend-Ausstellung," July 9, 10, 17, 1925.

"Hausmodelle aus der Jahresschau," July 16, 21, 23, 1925.

"Ausstellung von Gemälden alter Meister, Berliner Akademie der Künste," July 28, 1925.

"Deutsche Bildhauer der 13. Jahrhunderts: Die Skulpturen der Dome zu Strassburg, Bamberg, Naumburg," Oct. 20, 1925.

"Pechstein-Ausstellung bei Hugo Erfurth," Nov. 3, 1925.

"Das deutsche Kunstgewerbe in der Welt," Nov. 11, 1925.

"Deutsche Malerei des 19. und 20. Jahrhunderts: Ausstellung in der Galerie Arnold," Nov. 26, 1925.

"Wilhelm v. Bode," Dec. 10, 1925.

"Gegenreformation und Manierismus," * *Repertorium für Kunstwissenschaft*, 46 (1925), 243–62.

"Die Gemälde des Giovanni Battista Crespi genannt Cerano," *Jahrbuch der preussischen Kunstsammlungen*, 46 (1925), 259–85. Illus. *See also* "Nachtrag . . . ," 1928, below.

"Leipziger Barockhäuser, mit Eigenaufnahmen des Heimatschutzes," *Mitteilungen des Landesvereins Sächsischer Heimatschutz;* 14, pt. 7/8 (1925), 252–66. Illus.

* Reprinted in *Studies in Art, Architecture, and Design*, 1968.

"Neuerwerbungen italienischer Kunst in der Dresdner Gemälde-galerie," *Der Cicerone*, 17 (1925), 295–303. Pls. Illus.
"Die Neuordnung der Dresdner Gemäldegalerie," *Kunstwanderer*, Dec., 1925, pp. 142–44; Jan., 1926, p. 171. Illus.

1926

[Articles and reviews of exhibitions in Dresden], *Dresdner Anzeiger*, 1926:

"Paul Klee: Zur Ausstellung in der Galerie Arnold," 1926.

"Photographie als Kunst: I. Hugo Erfurth; II. Genja Jonas," 1926.

"Wassily Kandinsky: Jubiläumsausstellung in der Galerie Arnold," 1926.

"Otto Hettner: Januar-Ausstellung der Galerie Arnold," Jan., 1926.

"Max Slevogts Faust: Zur Ausstellung im Galerie Arnolds Graphischen Kabinett," Jan. 17, 1926.

"Jan Zrzavy: Zu der Gesamtausstellung im Graphischen Kabinett Hugo Erfurths," Jan. 23, 1926.

"Sonderausstellung Max Oppenheimer: Galerie Ernst Arnold," March 1, 1926.

"Max Feldbauer: Ausstellung im Graphischen Kabinett Hugo Erfurth," March 6, 1926.

"Maurice Utrillo: Ausstellung in der Galerie Arnold," March 25, 1926.

"Otto Dix: Ausstellung in der Galerie Arnold," April 6, 1926.

The remaining reviews for 1926 are concerned with the Internationale Kunstausstellung held in Dresden, 1926:

"Aus der Werkstatt der Internationalen Kunstausstellung," June 10, 1926.

"Rundgang durch die Internationale Kunstausstellung," June 13, 1926.

"Die französische Abteilung," June 18, 19, 1926.

"Spanien und Italien," June 29, 1926.

"Die nordische Abteilung," July, 1926.

"Belgien und Holland," July, 1926.

"England und Amerika," July 13, 1926.

"Tschechen, Polen und Ungarn," July 14, 1926.

"Russland," July 30, 1926.

"Die ältere deutsche Malerei," Aug. 7, 1926.

"Die deutsche Malerei der Gegenwart," Aug. –; Aug. 19, 1926.

"Dresdner Abteilung," Aug., 1926.

[Reviews and notices], *Cronache d'arte*, 3–5 (1926–28).

1927

[Articles and reviews of exhibitions in Dresden, etc.], *Dresdner Anzeiger*, 1927:

"Ausstellung der Akademie Dresden 1927: Staatliche Gemälde-galerie," 1927.

"Der Dresdner Maler Bernhard Kretzschmar: Zur Gesamtausstellung im Döbelner Stadtsmuseum," 1927.

"Dürerausstellung im Staatlichen Kupferstichkabinett," 1927.

"Liebermann-Ausstellungen im Staatlichen Kupferstichkabinett," 1927.

"Ludwig v. Hofmann: Ausstellung von Handzeichnungen in der Galerie Arnold," 1927.

"Munch-Ausstellung: Galerie Arnold," 1927.

"Otto Dix: Ausstellung in der Neuen Kunst Fides," 1927.

"Photographie als Kunst: Zur Ausstellung des Ateliers Riess in der Galerie Arnold," 1927.

"Sächsische Kunst unserer Zeit: Zweite Jubiläums-Ausstellung des Kunstvereins," 1927.

"Emil Nolde: Eröffnung der Jubiläums-Ausstellung im Städtischen Ausstellungsgebäude," Feb. 9, 19, 1927; March 11, 1927.

"Robert F. R. Scholtz: Ausstellung in der Galerie Arnold," March 16, 1927.

"Internationales Kunstgewerbe 1927: Ausstellung im Leipziger Grassi-Museum," March 17, 1927.

"Karl Schmidt-Rottluff: Aprilsausstellung in der Galerie Arnold," April, 1927.

"Von der Leipziger Internationalen Buchkunstausstellung," May, 1927.

"Moderne Graphik der Sammlung Dietel: Ausstellung in der Galerie Arnold, 26 bis 28 Sept.," Sept., 1927.

" 'Der Triumph der Amphitrite' von Tiepolo: Ein neu erworbenes Meisterwerk der Gemäldegalerie," Oct. 2, 1927.

"Ludwig v. Hofmann: Dezember-Ausstellung der Galerie Arnold," Dec., 1927.

"Die Galerie Ernst Arnold und das Dresdner Kunstleben," *Der Sammler*, Nov. 1, 1927, pp. 609–12. Illus.

"Die graphische Ausstellung des deutschen Künstlerbundes," *ibid.*, June 15, pp. 286–87. Illus.

"Eine Revision der Caravaggio-Daten," *Zeitschrift für bildende Kunst*, 61 (1927–28), 386–92.

1928

"Balthasar Permoser, der Bildhauer des Zwingers," *Dresdner Anzeiger*, 1928.

"Die Baugeschichte des Altstädter Rathauses zu Dresden," *Dresdner Geschichtsblätter*, 36, no. 1/2 (1928), 1–5. Illus. Plan.

"Beiträge zur Stilgeschichte des Früh- und Hochbarock," * *Repertorium für Kunstwissenschaft*, 49 (1928), 225–46.

"Die Lehrjahre des Caravaggio," *Zeitschrift für bildende Kunst*, 62 (1928–29), 278–88. Illus.

"Nachtrag zu Giovanni Battista Crespi genannt Cerano," *Jahrbuch der preussischen Kunstsammlungen*, 49 (1928), 48–49. Illus. *See also* "Die Gemälde des . . . Crespi . . . ," 1925, above.

1929

"Ein Altargemälde von Gentileschi in Turin," *Zeitschrift für bildende Kunst*, 63 (1929–30), 272–75. Illus.

"Das Altstädter Rathaus in Dresden und die Frage nach dem Schöpfer des Wiener Reichskanzleitraktes," *Zeitschrift für Denkmalpflege*, 3 (1929), 125–28. Illus. Plan.

"Giulio Cesare Procaccini," *Rivista d'arte*, anno 11 (ser. 2, anno 1) (July–Sept. 1929), pp. 321–54. Illus.

"Die Rokoko-Ausstellung in Venedig," *Zeitschrift für bildende Kunst*, 63 "Kunstchronik und Kunstliteratur" (Oct., 1929), 73–79. Illus.

"Über Dresdens Zukunft als Kunststadt. I. II," *Dresdner Anzeiger*, Jan., 1929.

* Reprinted in *Studies in Art, Architecture, and Design*, 1968.

1930

"Die Antwerpener Jahrhundert-Ausstellung," *Dresdner Anzeiger*, June 10, 1930.

1931

"Gemeinschaftsideale unter den bildenden Künstlern des 19. Jahrhunderts," *Deutsche Vierteljahrsschrift für Literaturwissenschaft und Geistesgeschichte*, Jahrg. 9 (1931), pp. 125–54.

1932

"Die Wandlung um 1650 in der italienischen Malerei," * *Wiener Jahrbuch für Kunstgeschichte*, 8 (22, 1932), 69–92. Illus.

1933

"Die Ausstellung der faschistischen Revolution," *Tägliche Rundschau* (Berlin), July 8, 1933.

"Die Bautätigkeit des Heiligen Godehard am Hildesheimer Dom," *Die Denkmalpflege: Zeitschrift für Denkmalpflege und Heimatschutz*, 1933, pp. 210–14. Illus. Plan.

"Die deutsche Kunst und die höheren Schulen," *Das Unterhaltungsblatt* (Berlin), April 3, 1933.

"Einige Regesten aus Akten der Florentiner Kunstakademie," *Mitteilungen des Kunsthistorischen Institutes in Florenz*, 4 (Jan.–July, 1933), 128–31.

"Fritz Schumacher," *Göttinger Tageblatt*, Feb. 16, 1933.

"Glückwünsche zum 50. Geburtstage des Wolkenkratzers," *Das Unterhaltungsblatt* (Berlin), Sept. 24, 1933.

"Kunstgeschichte in den Lehrplänen höherer Schulen," *Pädagogisches Zentralblatt*, 1933, pt. 4, pp. 179–82.

"Randbemerkungen zum Briefwechsel Furtwängler—Goebbels," [published by *Wolffsches Telegraphenbüro*, April 11, 1933], *Zeitwende*, 9 (July, 1933), 68–71.

* Reprinted in *Studies in Art, Architecture, and Design*, 1968.

"An Unknown Early Work of the School of Caravaggio," *Art in America,* 22 (Dec., 1933), 16–17. Pl. Tr. of "Ein unbekanntes Frühwerk des Michelangelo da Caravaggio," in *Festschrift für Walter Friedländer zum 60. Geburtstag am 10.3.1933.* [Typescript only.] A portrait of a young woman in the Cecconi collection, Florence.

1934

"Das Englische in der englischen Kunst: Die retrospektive Ausstellung britischer Kunst in der Londoner Akademie," *Deutsche Zukunft: Wochenzeitung für Politik Wirtschaft und Kultur,* 2 (Feb. 4, 1934), 15.

"James McNeill Whistler: Zum hundertsten Geburtstag," *Neue Zücher Zeitung,* July 10, 1934.

"Kunst und Staat," *Der Türmer,* March, 1934, pp. 514–17.

"Zur Kunst der Goethezeit: Übersicht über das Schrifttum des letzten Jahrzehntes," *Deutsche Vierteljahrsschrift für Literaturwissenschaft und Geistesgeschichte,* Jahrg. 12 (1934), pp. 306–27.

1935

"Birmingham Exhibition of Midland Art Treasures," *Burlington Magazine,* 66 (Jan., 1935), 30–35. Illus.

With Ethel Mairet. "Design and the Artist Craftsman.—2," *Design for Today,* 3 (June, 1935), 225–27.

"A Questionnaire on Industrial Art," *ibid.,* April, pp. 145–46.

1936

"The Designer in Industry," *Architectural Review,* 79–80 (1936). Illus.
  1. Carpets, April, pp. 185–90. Correspondence and reply by Nikolaus Pevsner, June, p. 300.
  2. Furnishing fabrics, June, pp. 291–96.
  3. Gas and electric fittings, July, pp. 45–48; Aug., pp. 87–90.
  4. Architectural metalwork, Sept., pp. 127–29.
  5. New materials and new processes, Oct., pp. 179–82.
  6. The role of the architect, Nov., pp. 227–30.

"Post-War Tendencies in German Art-Schools," *Journal of the Royal Society of Arts,* 84 (Jan. 17, 1936), 248–62.

Extract reprinted in *Design for Today,* Feb., 1936, pp. 78–80.

"Pottery: Design, Manufacture, Marketing," *Trend in Design,* Spring, 1936, pp. 9–19. Illus.

"Some Notes on Abraham Janssens," *Burlington Magazine,* 69 (Sept., 1936), 120–30. Pls.

"William Morris, C. R. Ashbee, und das zwanzigste Jahrhundert," *Deutsche Vierteljahrsschrift für Literaturwissenschaft und Geistesgeschichte,* Jahrg. 14 (1936), pp. 536–62.

> English tr.: "William Morris, C. R. Ashbee, and the Twentieth Century," *Manchester Review,* 7 (Winter, 1956), 437–58. Illus. Bibliog. Tr. by Evelyn Heaton.

1937

"C. F. A. Voysey: An Appreciation," *Architectural Review,* 82 (July, 1937), 360.

"Charles F. Annesley Voysey: Zum achtzigsten Geburtstage," *Deutsche Tapeten-Zeitung,* June 1, 1937.

> Reprinted in *Innendekoration,* 48 (June, 1937), pp. vii-viii.

"Clarendon Palace, eine Pfalz der englischen Könige," *Der Burgwart: Jahrbuch der Vereinigung zur Erhaltung deutscher Burgen für 1937,* Jahrg. 38, pp. 48–52. Illus. Plan.

"Design for Mass Production," *DIA News,* 1 (June, 1937).

"1860–1930," *Architectural Record,* 81 (March, 1937), 1–6. Illus. On architecture in England.

"Minor Masters of the XIXth Century; Christopher Dresser, Industrial Designer," *Architectural Review,* 81 (April, 1937), 183–86. Illus.

"Möbel von Gordon Russell—London," *Innendekoration,* 48 (Aug., 1937), 280–82. Illus.

"New Designs in Pottery and China," *Country Life,* Feb. 13, 1937, suppl. p. xxiv. Illus. Signed "L. Pevsner."

"Sperrholz als Bau- und Industriematerial," *Innendekoration,* 48 (May, 1937), pp. ii–iv.

1938

"English and German Art, and Their Inter-relations," *German Life and Letters,* o.s., 2 (July, 1938), 251–59. Bibliog.

"Fifty Years of Arts and Crafts," *Studio,* 116 (Nov., 1938), 225–30. Illus. A review by Nikolaus Pevsner and an early commentary by Bernard Shaw on the first Arts and Crafts exhibition, 1888, published in *The World,* Oct. 3, 1888.

"The First Plywood Furniture," *Architectural Review,* 84 (Aug., 1938), 75–76. Illus.

"Harlech und Beaumaris, der Höhepunkt britischer Burgenarchitektur," *Der Burgwart: Jahrbuch der Vereinigung zur Erhaltung deutscher Burgen für 1938,* Jahrg. 39, pp. 32–38. Illus. Plans.

"On the Furnishing of Girls' Schools: More Important in Its Implications than You May Think," *School and College Management,* 3 (Nov., 1938), 280–81. Illus.

"A Pioneer Designer: Arthur H. Mackmurdo," * *Architectural Review,* 83 (March, 1938), 141–43. Illus.

1939

"De academie voor beeldende kunsten en haar geschiedenis," *Elsevier's Maandschrift,* 49 (Jan., 1939), 15–29; (Feb., 1939), 95–101.

"Charles Rennie Mackintosh, 1869–1933: A Glasgow Pioneer of Modern Architecture," *Country Life,* 85 (April 15, 1939), 402–3. Illus.

"Danzig and Its Architecture," *ibid.,* May 20, pp. 521–24. Illus.

"An Exhibition of British Medieval Art," *Burlington Magazine,* 75 (July, 1939), 13–17. Illus. At the Burlington Fine Arts Club.

"Frank Lloyd Wright's Peaceful Penetration of Europe," *Architects' Journal,* May 4, 1939, pp. 731–34. Illus.

"George Walton, His Life and Work," * *Journal of the Royal Institute of British Architects,* 3rd ser., 46 (April 3, 1939), 537–48. Illus.

"The History of Plywood up to 1914," *Architectural Review,* 86 (Sept., 1939), 129–30.

"A Plea for Contemporary Craft," *DIA News,* 3 (June, 1939).

1940

"Broadcasting Comes of Age: The Radio Cabinet, 1919–1940," *Architectural Review,* 87 (May, 1940), 189–90.

* Reprinted in *Studies in Art, Architecture, and Design,* 1968.

"Charles F. Annesley Voysey," * Elsevier's Maandschrift, 50 (May, 1940), 343–55. Illus. Plans.

"Collections of Plaster Casts: The Example of the New Royal Academy of Art at the Hague," Museums Journal, 39 (Jan., 1940), 411–13. Illus.

"Design Parade," Studio, vols. 119–20 (1940), April, pp. 137–40; May, pp. 180–83; June, pp. 221–23; July, pp. 29–31. A review of industrial design.

"Style in Stamps: A Century of Postal Design," Country Life, 89 (May 4, 1940), pp. 464–65. Illus.

1941

"Bildhauer und Bildhauer-Zeichnungen," Die Zeitung (London), Nov. 17, 1941.

[Bruno Taut's career.] Architectural Review, 89 (June, 1941), 134–35.

"Charles F. Annesley Voysey, 1858–1941: A Tribute," ibid., May, pp. 112–13. Illus.

"Criticism," by Peter F. R. Donner [i.e., Nikolaus Pevsner], ibid., 90 (1941). Illus.:

1. "Frank Lloyd Wright: An Organic Architecture, the Architecture of Democracy. The Sir George Watson Lectures for 1939," Aug., pp. 68–70.

2. "Sir Herbert Baker's Extensions to the Bank of England," Sept., pp. 91–92.

3. "Ledoux and Le Corbusier," Oct., pp. 124–26.

4. "Houses by Robert Atkinson and the St. Marylebone Town Hall," Nov., pp. 151–52.

5. "Architecture in Germany under the Nazis," Dec., pp. 177–78.

"Englische Kunst und das Mittelmeer: Ausstellung im Warburg Institute," Die Zeitung (London), Dec. 18, 1941.

"Englische Künstler malen den Krieg: Ausstellung der War Artists in der National Gallery, von Peter Naumburg [i.e., Nikolaus Pevsner]," ibid., March 17.

"English Qualities in English Ceramics: Evolution Rather than Revolution," Country Life, 90 (Oct. 3, 1941), 625. Illus.

"English Qualities in English Glass," ibid., July 19, p. 109. Illus.

* Reprinted in Studies in Art, Architecture, and Design, 1968.

"A Giambologna Statuette in Mr. F. D. Lycett Green's Collection," *Burling-ton Magazine*, 78 (Jan., 1941), 22–27.

"Kinderkunst, von Peter Naumburg [i.e., Nikolaus Pevsner]," *Die Zeitung* (London), Aug. 22, 1941.

"Meine Kollegen, die Schuttschipper, von Ramaduri [i.e., Nikolaus Pevs-ner]," *ibid.*, Sept. 1.

"Omega," *Architectural Review*, 90 (Aug., 1941), 45–48. Illus. On Roger Fry and the Omega Workshops.

Letter, signed Peter F. R. Bonner [*sic*], *ibid.*, Sept., p. xxxiv.

"Schuttschipper-Psychologie," *Die Zeitung* (London), Sept. 25, 1941.

"Whistler's 'Valparaiso Harbour' at the Tate Gallery," *Burlington Magazine*, 79 (Oct., 1941), 115–21. Pl.

1942

"A. H. Mackmurdo," *Journal of the Royal Institute of British Architects*, 3rd ser., 49 (April, 1942), 94–95. A note on Mackmurdo's acquaintance with James McNeill Whistler.

"A Bronze Statuette by Peter Vischer the Elder," *Burlington Magazine*, 80 (April, 1942), 90–93. Pls.

"The Evolution of the Easy Chair," *Architectural Review*, 91 (March, 1942), 59–62. Illus.

"Heritage of Compromise: A Note on Sir Joshua Reynolds Who Died One Hundred and Fifty Years Ago," *ibid.*, Feb., pp. 37–38. Illus.

[Letter to the editor on R. P. Ross Williamson's article "Victorian Necrop-olis: The Cemeteries of London," in *ibid.*, Oct.], *ibid.*, 92 (Nov., 1942), xxxiv–xxxvi.

"Mr. Pevsner Remembers Mackmurdo," *Architects' Journal*, April 16, 1942, pp. 274–75. On Arthur H. Mackmurdo.

"Nine Swallows—No Summer," *Architectural Review*, 91 (May, 1942), 109–12. Illus. On certain early twentieth-century buildings in Britain.

"Patient Progress: The Life Work of Frank Pick," * *ibid.*, 92 (Aug., 1942), 31–48. Illus.

[Short reviews of London exhibitions, etc.], *Die Zeitung* (London), May–July, 1942.

"Walter Richard Sickert," Jan. 30, 1942.

"150 Jahre englischer Malerei," Feb. 24, 1942.

* Reprinted in *Studies in Art, Architecture, and Design*, 1968.

"Das Bild des Monats," Feb. 24, April 10, May 29, June 26, July 17, 1942.

"Englische Kathedralen," May 15, 1942.

"Londoner Kunstausstellungen," May 22, 1942.

"Alte und neue Plastik," July 31, 1942.

"Londoner Ausstellungen," Oct. 23, 1942.

"The Term 'Architect' in the Middle Ages," *Speculum,* 17 (Oct., 1942), 549–62.

    Abstracted in *American Journal of Archaeology,* 47 (July, 1943), 341–42.

"Terms of Architectural Planning in the Middle Ages," *Journal of the Warburg and Courtauld Institutes,* 5 (1942), 232–37.

"Treasure Hunt: Critical Notes by Peter F. R. Donner [i.e., Nikolaus Pevsner]," *Architectural Review,* 91, 92 (1942). Illus. On nineteenth-century buildings in and around London.

    1. Bishopsgate, Jan., pp. 23–25.

    2. Eton College Estate, N.W. 3., Feb., pp. 47–49.

    3. Parliament Square, March, pp. 75–77.

    4. Houses in South Wimbledon, May, pp. 123–24.

    5. Houses in Eton Avenue, N.W. 3., June, pp. 151–53.

    6. Tenement houses, Westminster, July, pp. 19–21.

    7. Parkside, Wimbledon Common, Aug., pp. 49–51.

    8. Houses in Golders Green, Sept., pp. 75–76.

    9. Army and Navy Stores, Victoria St., S.W. 1., Oct., pp. 97–99.

    10. Houses between Morden and Cheam, Surrey, Nov., pp. 125–26.

    11. Insurance offices in the City, Dec., pp. 151–53.

"Works and Planning: The New Ministry's Multiple Tasks, Research for Reconstruction, from a Correspondent," *Times,* Nov. 18, 1942.

1943

"The End of the Pattern Books, by Peter F. R. Donner [i.e., Nikolaus Pevsner]," *Architectural Review,* 93 (March, 1943), 75–79. Illus. Plan.

"A Harris Florilegium, by Peter F. R. Donner [i.e., Nikolaus Pevsner]," *ibid.,* Feb., pp. 51–52. On Thomas Harris, *Victorian Architecture* (1860).

"The Lure of Rusticity, by Peter F. R. Donner [i.e., Nikolaus Pevsner]," *ibid.*, Jan., p. 270. Illus. On Paul Decker, *Gothic Architecture Decorated* (1759).

"Model Houses for the Labouring Classes," * *ibid.*, May, pp. 119–28. Illus. Plans. Compiled by Nikolaus Pevsner.

"Review of the Exhibition," *Architectural Association Journal*, 58 (April, 1943), 82–83. An exhibition of the work of the students of the Architectural Association.

"A Short Pugin Florilegium," *Architectural Review*, 94 (Aug., 1943), 31–34. Illus. Compiled by Nikolaus Pevsner.

1944

"Edensor, or Brown Comes True," *Architectural Review*, 95 (Feb., 1944), 39–43. On Richard Brown, *Domestic Architecture* (1841) and the village of Edensor, Derbyshire.

"The Genesis of the Picturesque," * *ibid.*, 96 (Nov., 1944), 139–46. Illus. Bibliog.

"Homes of the Future," *Europe* (A Staples publication), 1944, p. 58.

"Mannerism and Architecture," *Architectural Review*, 96 (Dec., 1944), 184. With special reference to Niccolò dell'Abbate.

"Price on Picturesque Planning," * *ibid.*, 95 (Feb., 1944), 47–50. A summary of Sir Uvedale Price, *An Essay on the Picturesque* (1810).

"Questionnaire: Design in the Pottery Industry," *Pottery and Glass*, Nov., 1944, pp. 8–13; Dec., 1944, pp. 7–13.

1945

With Geoffrey Grigson. "The *Architectural Review* Gothic Number: Act 2: Romantic Gothic: Scene I: Goethe and Strassburg," *Architectural Review*, 98 (Dec., 1954), 156–59. Illus. A translation, with marginal commentary by Nikolaus Pevsner, of Goethe's *Von deutscher Baukunst*.

"Artists and Academies," *Listener*, May 31, 1945, pp. 607–8.

"Can Painters Design Fabrics?" *Harper's*, Nov., 1945, pp. 27–30. Illus.

"Thoughts on Henry Moore," *Burlington Magazine*, 86 (Feb., 1945), 47–49.

* Reprinted in *Studies in Art, Architecture, and Design*, 1968.

"Visual Planning and the City of London," *Architects' Journal*, Dec. 13, 1945, p. 440. A paper read before the Architectural Association, Nov. 27, 1945. Discussion.

> Reprinted in *Architectural Association Journal*, 61 (Dec., 1945—Jan., 1946), 31–36.

1946

"Bombed Churches as War Memorials," *Listener*, May 16, 1946, p. 639. Illus. Extract from a broadcast talk.

"Henry Moore's Madonna [at St. Matthew's, Northampton]," *The Student Movement*, Oct., 1946, pp. 4–5. Illus.

"Target for September: Nikolaus Pevsner Urges Manufacturers to Aim High in the Quality of Their Designs for the 'Britain Can Make It' Exhibition," *Pottery and Glass*, May, 1946, p. 17.

"Thoughts on Industrial Design," *The Highway: Journal of the Workers' Educational Association*, March, 1946, pp. 70–71.

1947

"An Eighteenth-Century 'Improver': Nikolaus Pevsner on Richard Payne Knight," *Listener*, Jan. 30, 1947, pp. 204–5. Illus.

"Greece, Rome—and Washington: Nikolaus Pevsner on the Need for a New Style in Monumental Architecture," *ibid.*, July 17, pp. 93–94. Illus.

"Merchandise Design and Retail Selling," *Store, Magazine of Retailing*, 11 (Aug., 1947), 18–20.

"Modern Architecture and Tradition," *The Highway: Journal of the Workers' Educational Association*, Aug., 1947, pp. 228–32. Illus.

"Notre Dame de France," *Architectural Review*, 101 (March, 1947), 111. Illus. On the former church of Notre Dame de France, Leicester Place, London, by L. A. Boileau, 1868.

"The Other Chambers," *ibid.*, June, pp. 195–98. Illus. On Sir William Chambers, *Dissertation on Oriental Gardening* (1773).

"The Picturesque in Architecture," *Journal of the Royal Institute of British Architects*, 3rd ser., 55 (Dec., 1947), 55–61. Illus. Read before the Royal Institute of British Architects, Nov. 25, 1947.

1948

With S. Land. "Apollo or Baboon," *Architectural Review*, 104 (Dec., 1948), 271–79. Illus. On the Greek Doric Revival.

"Bruegel's 'The Adoration of the Kings.' I. The Painter's Message," *Listener*, Feb. 5, 1948, pp. 215–16. Illus.

"Design in Relation to Industry through the Ages," * *Journal of the Royal Society of Arts*, 97 (Dec. 31, 1948), 90–100. Cobb Lecture, Nov. 24, 1948.

"Foreign Trends in Design and Their Effect in This Country," *Architects' Journal*, Dec. 2, 1948, p. 514. Talks at the Design and Industries Association by Nikolaus Pevsner and Misha Black, Nov. 3, 1948.

"Humphry Repton: A Florilegium," *Architectural Review*, 103 (Feb., 1948), 53–59. Illus. Plans.

"Monsù Desiderio, a Little-Known Precursor of Rococo and Gothick," *ibid.*, 104 (Sept., 1948), 149. Bibliog. On François de Nomé, called Francisco Desiderio. See article by A. Scharf, *ibid.*, 105 (Feb., 1949), 91–94.

"Der Monumentalbau in unserer Welt," *Blick in die Welt*, 1948, no. 20, pp. 13–15. Illus.

"North Wilts Church Magazine," *Architects' Journal*, Dec. 16, 1948, p. 552. Letter on Canon Bertrand Pleydell Bouverie.

"The Painting and Sculpture of Denmark," *Listener*, Nov. 25, 1948, pp. 808–9. Illus.

"The Saga of the Dukeries," *ibid.*, Nov. 11, pp. 718–20. Illus. On Welbeck, Thoresby, Clumber, and Worksop.

"Stuart and Georgian Churches," *Times Literary Supplement*, March 27, 1948, p. 177; April 17, 1948, p. 219. Letters to the editor on the review of Marcus Whiffen, *Stuart and Georgian Churches* (London, 1947, 1948).

1949

"Early Iron: 2. Curvilinear Hothouses," *Architectural Review*, 106 (Sept., 1949), 188–89. Plans.

"The First Cambridge Slade Professor: Nikolaus Pevsner on Sir Matthew

* Reprinted in *Studies in Art, Architecture, and Design*, 1968.

Digby Wyatt," *Listener,* Nov. 10, 1949, pp. 807–9. Illus. An abridged version of the inaugural lecture.

"From William Morris to Walter Gropius: Nikolaus Pevsner Gives the First of Three Talks on the Bauhaus," *ibid.,* March 17, pp. 439–40. Illus.

"German Painting of the Age of Reformation," *ibid.,* Aug. 4, pp. 181–82. Illus.

"Reassessment 4. Three Oxford Colleges," *Architectural Review,* 106 (Aug., 1949), 120–24. Illus. Christ Church, Corpus Christi, and St. Edmund Hall.

"Richard Payne Knight," * *Art Bulletin,* 31 (Dec., 1949), 293–320.

With S. Lang. "Sir William Temple and Sharawaggi," *Architectural Review,* 106 (Dec., 1949), 391–93. Illus. Bibliog.

"Surrealism in the Sixteenth Century," *ibid.,* p. 399. Illus. On a painting by Giuseppe Arcimboldi.

1950

"Double Profile: A Reconsideration of the Elizabethan Style as Seen at Wollaton," *Architectural Review,* 107 (March, 1950), 147–53. Illus. Plans.

"Goethe and Architecture," *Listener,* Jan. 19, 1950, pp. 103–4, Illus.

"Good King James's Gothic," * *Architectural Review,* 107 (Feb., 1950), 117–22. Illus. Plans. On the Jacobean revival of the eighteenth and nineteenth centuries.

"Notebooks of a Master Mason: Nikolaus Pevsner on Villard de Honnecourt," *Listener,* March 2, 1950, pp. 379–80. Illus.

"Privacy and the Flat: Venetian Solutions," *Architectural Review,* 107 (May, 1950), 351–53.

"Revivalisms in Architecture," *Listener,* June 22, 1950, pp. 1054–57. Illus. Aspects of art in England.

"The Training of Architects: Interim Survey," *Architectural Review,* 107 (June, 1950), 367–73. Illus. Compiled on the basis of a questionnaire sent to schools of architecture in 14 countries.

"Visual Aspects of the Cambridge Plan," *Cambridge Review,* May 13, 1950, pp. 510–13. On William Holford and Henry Myles Wright, *Cambridge Planning Proposals* (1950).

* Reprinted in *Studies in Art, Architecture, and Design,* 1968.

1951

"Baroque Painting in Italy," *Listener,* Feb. 1, 1951, pp. 171–73. Illus.
"The Burgundian Exhibition in Brussels," *ibid.,* Dec. 6, pp. 965–67. Illus.
"Canons of Criticism," *Architectural Review,* 109 (Jan., 1951), 3–6. A commentary on the Coventry Cathedral competition and certain letters to the *Times.*

> Letter, and comments by Nikolaus Pevsner, *Architectural Review,* 109 (March, 1951), p. 196.

> Spanish tr.: *Cánones de la crítica,* 1954.

"COID: Progress Report. Industrial Design: 1951," *Architectural Review,* 110 (Dec., 1951), 353–59. Illus. An examination of the exhibits chosen by the Council of Industrial Design for the South Bank exhibition.
"Early Cast-Iron Façades," *ibid.,* 109 (June, 1951), 398. Letter to the editors in connection with Professor H.-R. Hitchcock's article in *ibid.,* Feb.
"Hans Dietrich Gronau," *Kunstchronik,* 4 (May, 1951), 122. Obituary.
"Il Festival di Londra," *Communità,* Oct. 12, 1951, pp. 48–51.
"Goethe e l'architettura," * *Palladio: Rivista di storia dell'architettura,* n.s., anno 1 (Oct.–Dec., 1951), pp. 174–79.
"How to Judge Victorian Architecture," *Listener,* July 19, 1951, pp. 91–92.
"The Late Victorians and William Morris," *ibid.,* Aug. 9, pp. 217–19. Illus.
"Victorian Churches and Public Buildings," *ibid.,* Aug. 2, pp. 177–79.
"Victorian Thought on Architecture," *ibid.,* July 26, pp. 137–39. Illus.

1952

"Another Furness Building," *Architectural Review,* 112 (Sept., 1952), 196. Illus. On the Provident Life and Trust Co. building, Philadelphia, by Frank Furness, 1879.
"Art Furniture of the Eighteen-Seventies," * *ibid.,* 111 (Jan., 1952), 43–50. Illus.
"Bolsover Castle" *Derbyshire Countryside,* 19 (Oct.–Dec., 1952), 78–79. Illus.
"The Cambridge Campus of the Future," *Cambridge Review,* April 19, 1952, pp. 391–92.

* Reprinted in *Studies in Art, Architecture, and Design,* 1968.

"Englishmen's Castles: Bolsover Castle, Derbyshire," *Listener*, July 3, 1952, pp. 14–16. Illus.

"Englishmen's Castles: Lumley Castle, County Durham," *ibid.*, June 26, pp. 1033–34. Illus.

> Summary reprinted as "Lumley Castle," *London Calling*, Aug. 6, 1953, pp. 9, 12. Illus.

"Englishmen's Castles: Strawberry Hill, Twickenham," *Listener*, July 10, 1952, pp. 55–56. Illus.

> Summary reprinted as "Strawberry Hill Gothic," *London Calling*, Oct. 29, 1953, pp. 10–11. Illus.

"National Collection of Photography," *Times*, June 28, 1952. Letter by Nikolaus Pevsner, Lucia Moholy, and Tom Hopkinson.

"Once More Leonardo da Vinci," *Architectural Review*, 112 (Aug., 1952), 126. Illus. Translation of an application by Leonardo to Sultan Bajezid II to build a bridge from Pera to Constantinople.

"Pioneer of the Pedestrian Network," *ibid.*, July, p. 57. Illus. On a Leonardo da Vinci drawing: Institut de France, Codex B, 16r.

"Schinkel," * *Journal of the Royal Institute of British Architects*, 3rd ser., 59 (Jan., 1952), 89–96. Illus. Paper read before the Royal Institute of British Architects, Dec. 11, 1951.

"Shaw of Wellington," *Architectural Review*, 111 (June, 1952), 416–17. Illus. On John Shaw (1803–70), architect of Wellington College, Berks.

"The Strange Architecture of Antonio Gaudí," *Listener*, Aug. 7, 1952, pp. 213–14. Illus.

"Study of Art History," *Times*, Nov. 5, 1952. Letter.

> Letters by R. H. Wilenski, A. F. Blunt, *ibid.*, Nov. 7; letter by Percy Horton, Nov. 8; reply by Nikolaus Pevsner, Nov. 13.

"Thoughts on Coventry Cathedral," *Listener*, Jan. 17, 1952, pp. 94–96. Illus.

"Tintoretto and Mannerism," *Architectural Review*, 111 (June, 1952), 361–65. Illus.

> Letter by E. Newton; reply by Nikolaus Pevsner, *ibid.*, 112 (Sept., 1952), 203.

"An Un-English Activity. I. Reflections on Not Teaching Art History," *Listener*, Oct. 30, 1952, pp. 715–16.

> Comment: "Art and Science," *ibid.*, p. 710. Leading article.

"Victorian and Edwardian Design," *Architectural Review*, 112 (Dec.,

* Reprinted in *Studies in Art, Architecture, and Design*, 1968.

1952), 401–3. Illus. On the exhibition at the Victoria and Albert Museum, London.

1953

"Bristol, Troyes, Gloucester: The Character of the Early Fourteenth Century in Architecture," *Architectural Review*, 113 (Feb., 1953), 88–98. Illus. Plan.

Letter by Brian Little, *ibid.*, 114 (Sept., 1953), 141–42.

"British Museum: Some Unsolved Problems of Its Architectural History," *ibid.*, 113 (March, 1953), 179–82. Illus. Plan.

Letter by Maurice Craig, *ibid.*, 114 (Oct., 1953), 282. Illus.

"Colonel Gillum and the Pre-Raphaelites," *Burlington Magazine*, 95 (March, 1953), 78–81. Pls.

"Good Luck to Bad Art," *Granta*, 61 (Feb. 7, 1953), 9–10.

"Johannesburg: The Development of a Contemporary Vernacular in the Transvaal," *Architectural Review*, 113 (June, 1953), 361–82. Illus. Plans.

"A Pilgrims' Church," *Listener*, Dec. 31, 1953, pp. 1120–22. Illus. Sainte Foy, Conques.

"The Sidgwick Avenue Site [i.e., for Cambridge University buildings]," *Cambridge Review*, Oct. 31, 1953, pp. 88–89.

1954

"Arts, Manufactures, and Commerce, 1754–1954," *Journal of the Royal Society of Arts*, 102, Bicentenary Issue II (April 16, 1954), 392–405. The three Bicentenary Lectures: I. The Arts. By Nikolaus Pevsner, March 23, 1954.

Extract reprinted in *Scotsman*, March 24, 1954.

"Dam-building in the Dolomites," *Listener*, Dec. 9, 1954, pp. 1007–8. Illus.

"John Wood at Llandaff," *Architectural Review*, 115 (June, 1954), 411–12. Illus. On the partial rebuilding of Llandaff cathedral by John Wood the Elder.

"Old Somerset House," *ibid.*, 116 (Sept., 1954), 163–67. Illus. Plans.

"Rosa Schapire," *Kunstchronik*, 7 (April, 1954), 111. Obituary.

"The Royal Society of Arts after 200 Years," *Listener*, March 25, 1954, pp. 521, 533.

"Sir Christopher Wren," *Proceedings of the Royal Institution of Great Britain*, 35 (1954), 734–39. Plans. Paper read March 19, 1954.

"Towers in the City? I Say Yes," *Evening Standard*, Nov. 24, 1954. On tower blocks in the City of London.

"Twentieth-Century Picturesque: An Answer to Basil Taylor's Broadcast" [on "English Art and the Picturesque"], *Architectural Review*, 115 (April, 1954), 227–29. Illus.

> Letter by Basil Taylor and a reply by Nikolaus Pevsner, *ibid.*, May, p. 364.

> Letter by A. I. T. Colquhoun and a reply by Nikolaus Pevsner, *ibid.*, 116 (July, 1954), 2.

1955

"Design Review: German Church Furnishings," *Architectural Review*, 118 (Oct., 1955), 270–73. Illus.

> Letter by Frances Rumbold, *ibid.*, 119 (Jan., 1956), 2.

"The Englishness of English Art: BBC Reith Lectures," *Listener*, Oct.–Dec., 1955.

> 1. "The Geography of Art," Oct. 20, pp. 643–44.
> 2. "Hogarth and Observed Life," Oct. 27, pp. 693–95.
> 3. "Sir Joshua Reynolds and Detachment," Nov. 3, pp. 735–37.
> 4. "Perpendicular England," Nov. 10, pp. 781–83.
> 5. "Blake and the Flaming Line," Nov. 17, pp. 834–35.
> 6. "Constable and the Pursuit of Nature," Nov. 24, pp. 883–85.
> 7. "The Genius of the Place," Dec. 1, pp. 931–33.

> Letter by Hugh Plommer, *ibid.*, Nov. 10, pp. 803–5; reply by Nikolaus Pevsner, Nov. 17, p. 855; reply by Plommer, Nov. 24, p. 899; reply by Pevsner, Dec. 1, p. 941; reply by Plommer, Dec. 8, p. 1007.

> Letter by Douglas Cooper, *ibid.*, Nov. 24, p. 899; reply by Alec Clifton-Taylor, Dec. 1, p. 941.

> Summaries in *Times*, Oct. 17, 24, 31, Nov. 7, 14, 21, 28, 1955.

> Published, 1956, in book form, revised.

> Comment: "English Art," *Times*, Nov. 28, 1955. Leading article. Letter by Bertram Hume, *Listener*, Dec. 8, 1955, p. 1007.

"Excavations," *Architectural Review*, 117 (March, 1955), 195. On the need for an organized service for the excavation of mediaeval sites in Britain.

"Hill Hall," *ibid.*, May, pp. 307–9. Illus. On Hill Hall, Essex.

[Letter on Gothic survival and revival in reply to an article by R. Bernheimer, *Art Bulletin*, Dec., 1954], *Art Bulletin*, 37 (Sept., 1955), 235.

"No Grace for Mackintosh," *Architectural Review*, 118 (Aug., 1955), 117–18. On the Ingram Street tearooms, Glasgow.

" 'Rococo Art from Bavaria' in London," *Kunstchronik*, 8 (Jan., 1955), 5–7. Review of an exhibition, Victoria and Albert Museum, London, Oct.–Dec., 1954.

"William Morris Society," *Times*, Sept. 13, 1955. Letter by J. Brandon-Jones, Stanley Morison, and Nikolaus Pevsner.

1956

"The Birkbeck War Memorial: Three Opinions. 3. The War Memorial," *Lodestone* (Birkbeck College, University of London), 47 (Spring and Summer, 1956), 9–12. On a statue by Ralph Beyer.

With S. Lang. "The Egyptian Revival," * *Architectural Review*, 119 (May, 1956), 242–54. Illus.

Letter by John Harris, *ibid.*, 122 (July, 1957), 2.

"Englische Architektur zur Zeit Shakespeares," *Kunstchronik*, 9 (Oct., 1956), 278–79. Summary of a lecture, Sechster Deutscher Kunsthistorikertag, Essen, Aug. 1–4, 1956.

"Fischer von Erlach, 1656–1723," *Architectural Review*, 120 (Oct., 1956), 215–17. Illus.

"The Imperial College: A New Start on a New Site," *Times*, Feb. 27, 1956. Letter.

"On Finding Oneself Out of Date. Men of the Year: Nikolaus Pevsner," *Architects' Journal*, Jan. 19, 1956, pp. 76–88. On the Modern Movement and contemporary architecture.

"A Setting for St. Paul's Cathedral," *Listener*, May 10, 1956, pp. 594–96. Illus.

"Topography: Frith and the Irregular," *Architectural Review*, 120 (Sept., 1956), 191. Illus. On the buildings depicted in William Frith's *Ramsgate Sands*.

"Welcome to Professor Martin," *Cambridge Review*, Nov. 10, 1956, pp. 136–37. Illus. On Dr. Leslie Martin's appointment as professor of architecture at Cambridge University.

* Reprinted in *Studies in Art, Architecture, and Design*, 1968.

"The Work of Walter Gropius, Royal Gold Medallist 1956," *Journal of the Royal Institute of British Architects*, 3rd ser., 63 (April, 1956), 228–31. Illus. Speeches by Nikolaus Pevsner and others.

> Extracts reprinted as "Dr. Gropius: England's Second Friendly Welcome," *Architects' Journal*, April 26, 1956, p. 373.

1957

"Architecture and William Morris," * *Journal of the Royal Institute of British Architects*, 3rd ser., 64 (March, 1957), 172–77. Read at the Royal Institute of British Architects, Feb. 19, 1957.

"Berlin, City of Tomorrow," *Listener*, Aug. 8, 1957, pp. 197–99. Illus.

"Bohemian Hawksmoor," *Architectural Review*, 121 (Feb., 1957), 112–14. Illus. On Giovanni Santini Aichel.

"George Stubbs: Rückblick auf eine Londoner Ausstellung," *Neue Zürcher Zeitung*, April 15, 1957. An exhibition held at the Whitechapel Gallery.

"Glass Skyscrapers," *Architectural Review*, 122 (Nov., 1957), 294. Illus. Letter to the editors on early projects of Ludwig Hilberseimer, quoting a letter by Hilberseimer.

[Introduction.] "Report of a Debate on the Motion 'That Systems of Proportion Make Good Design Easier and Bad Design More Difficult,' Held at the Royal Institute of British Architects on 18 June. Dr. Nikolaus Pevsner Introduced the Subject," *Journal of the Royal Institute of British Architects*, 3rd ser., 64 (Sept., 1957), 456–63. Illus. Plans.

"An Italian Miscellany: Pedrocchino and Some Allied Problems," *Architectural Review*, 122 (Aug., 1957), 112–15. Illus. Bibliog. On the Caffè Pedrocchi and the Pedrocchino, Padua, both by Giuseppe Jappelli.

"Pleinair-Plastik in London," *Neue Zürcher Zeitung*, July 19, 1957. On the London County Council sculpture exhibition in Holland Park.

"Universities: 1. Yesterday," *Architectural Review*, 122 (Oct., 1957), 234–39. Illus.

> Italian tr.: "Le università: ieri," *Architettura Cantiere*, 20 (March, 1959), 5–10, Illus.

"An Unknown Statue by Nicolaus Gerhaert," *Burlington Magazine*, 99 (Feb., 1957), 40–41. Illus. A Virgin and Child in wood at Downside Abbey.

"Weissenhof," *Architectural Review*, 122 (Dec., 1957), 414–15. Illus. Plan. On the Weissenhof-Siedlung, Stuttgart.

* Reprinted in *Studies in Art, Architecture, and Design*, 1968.

1958

"Backyard Mentality," *Architectural Review*, 124 (Dec., 1958), 409–12. Illus. On the Warburg Institute building, University of London.

"Churchill College—Some Considerations: Passions Not Aroused," *Varsity* (Cambridge), May 17, 1958, pp. 6–7.

"Dr. Pevsner Broadcasts: Architecture in New Zealand, New Architecture and New Art, Towns and Traditions," *Journal of the New Zealand Institute of Architects*, 25 (Nov., 1958), 257–65.

> Reprinted in *New Zealand Listener*, Dec. 12, Dec. 26, 1958.

"Georgian Sculptors: Victor Alexander Sederbach," *Architectural Review*, 123 (May, 1958), 332–34. Illus.

"The Hotel Room," *Observer*, May 11, 1958. Letter on the shortcomings of hotel furnishing.

"The Ingratiating Chaos: Impressions of New Zealand," *Listener*, Nov. 20, 1958, pp. 825–27. Illus.

> Letter by J. A. W. Bennett, *ibid.*, Dec. 4, p. 934.

> Extract reprinted in *Journal of the New Zealand Institute of Architects*, 26 (March, 1959), 42–43.

> Comment by F. E. Greenish, *ibid.*, pp. 43–50.

"King Ramiro's Churches [in Asturias, Spain]," *Listener*, March 20, 1958, pp. 493–95. Illus.

"A Liturgical Brief," *Architectural Review*, 124 (Oct., 1958), 212. Letter to the editors on Rudolf Schwartz, quoting from an article of his in *Werk und Zeit*, May, 1958.

"The Three Dimensional Arch from the Sixteenth to the Eighteenth Century," *Journal of the Society of Architectural Historians*, 17 (Winter, 1958), 22–24. Illus. Plan.

"Das Zeitalter Ludwigs XIV: Ausstellung in der Royal Academy, London," *Neue Zürcher Zeitung*, Jan. 24, 1958.

1959

"Commonwealth I," *Architectural Review*, 126 (Oct., 1959), 149–217. Illus. On modern architecture in Canada, South Africa, Australia, and New Zealand.

Letters by W. Duncan Howie and I. B. Reynolds, *ibid.*, 127 (March, 1960), 155.

Comments on the section on New Zealand architecture by Alan Wild, *New Zealand Listener*, Feb. 12, 1960, pp. 6–7. Letter in reply by Nikolaus Pevsner, *ibid.*, March 25.

Reprinted *in* J. M. Richards. *New Buildings in the Commonwealth.* 1961.

"Italian Prisoners of War Memorial," *Architectural Review*, 125 (Feb., 1959), 139–40. Illus. Memorial at Mauthausen, designed by Mario Labò.

"Marney's Gatehouse," *Listener*, Nov. 19, 1959, p. 862. Illus. Extract from a broadcast talk on Layer Marney, Essex.

"Das neue Coventry," *Stuttgarter Zeitung*, Feuilleton, Dec. 19, 1959.

"A Note on the East End of Winchester Cathedral," *Archaeological Journal*, 116 (1959), 133–35. Illus.

Reprinted in *Winchester Cathedral Record*, 1960, pp. 7–10. Pls.

"Roehampton: LCC Housing and the Picturesque Tradition," *Architectural Review*, 126 (July, 1959), 21–35. Illus.

"Romantik Ausstellung," *Schweizer Monatshefte*, 39 (Sept., 1959), 554–57. On the Council of Europe Romantic Exhibition in London.

"Roots and Branches: The Story of Sir Gordon Russell's Development of Industrial Design," *Design*, no. 132 (Dec., 1959), 28–35. Illus.

"Schweizer Kunst in London," *Neue Zürcher Zeitung*, Nov. 3, 1959. On the Arts Council's and Pro Helvetia's exhibitions at the Tate Gallery and the Royal Institute of British Architects, London.

"The Study of Art History [at Oxford and Cambridge Universities]," *Times*, Nov. 5, 1959. Letter.

"Time and Le Corbusier," *Architectural Review*, 125 (March, 1959), 159–65. Illus. A plea for the preservation of Le Corbusier's early works.

German tr.: "Die Zeit und Le Corbusier," *Deutsche Bauzeitung*, 65 (July, 1960), 367–72. Illus.

"The Value of History to Students of Architecture," *Architects' Journal*, April 23, 1959, p. 639. Statements by Nikolaus Pevsner and others.

1960

" 'Argentinian Edwardian' in Córdoba," *Listener*, Dec. 29, 1960, p. 1182.

"Change at Euston," *Times*, April 19, 1960. Letter on Euston Station.

"Gaudí—Pioneer or Outsider," *Architects' Journal,* 132 (Dec. 15, 1960), 852.

"Ince Blundell Pantheon," *Times,* April 8, 1960. Letter by Nikolaus Pevsner and others.

[Letter to the editors on Balthasar Neumann's copy of *Vitruvius Britannicus* and the plan of the Bishop's Palace at Würzburg], *Architectural Review,* 128 (Sept., 1960), 239. Plans.

"1960: Propositions: 5. The Editors, J. M. Richards, Nikolaus Pevsner, Hugh Casson, and H. de C. Hastings Review the Trend of the Series [Architecture after 1960: Propositions]," *ibid.,* 127 (June, 1960), 381–88.

[Obituary: C. H. Holden, 1874–1960], *ibid.,* 128 (Dec., 1960), 446–48. Illus.

"Obituary: Sir Giles [Gilbert] Scott," *ibid.,* 127 (June, 1960), 424–26.

"Old Buildings at Eltham," *Listener,* Jan. 21, 1960, p. 118. Extract from a broadcast talk on Eltham Palace and Eltham Lodge.

"Peter Floud, 1911–60," *Architectural Review,* 127 (March, 1960), 154. Obituary.

"Sources of Art in the Twentieth Century: Nikolaus Pevsner on the Exhibition in Paris Organized by the Council of Europe," *Listener,* Dec. 8, 1960, pp. 1042–44. Illus.

1961

"The Art of Ernst Barlach," *Listener,* May 25, 1961, p. 934. Illus.

"Burlington-Devonshire Drawings," *Architectural Review,* 129 (May, 1961), 299.

"Dark Gold: Nikolaus Pevsner on a Baroque Town in Brazil," *Listener,* Jan. 19, 1961, p. 135. Illus. On Ouro Preto.

With John Harris. "John Bodt in England," *Architectural Review,* 130 (July, 1961), 29–34. Illus.

"Lethaby's Last," *ibid.,* Nov., pp. 354–57. Illus. On W. R. Lethaby's church at Brockhampton, Herefordshire.

"Libraries 1: Nutrimentum Spiritus," *ibid.,* Oct., 240–44. Illus. Plan.
    Reprinted in *Lucknow Librarian,* 2 (March, 1964), 202–8.

"London Revisited," *Vogue,* Feb. 15, 1961, pp. 45, 102, 104.

"Modern Architecture and the Historian, or the Return of Historicism," *

* Reprinted in *Studies in Art, Architecture, and Design,* 1968.

Journal of the Royal Institute of British Architects, 3rd ser., 68 (April, 1961), 230–40. Illus. A lecture given at the Royal Institute of British Architects on Jan. 10, 1961.

> Broadcast version printed as "The Return of Historicism in Architecture," *Listener*, Feb. 16, 1961, pp. 299–301.

> German tr. "Moderne Architektur und der Historiker oder, die Wiederkehr des Historismus," *Deutsche Bauzeitung*, 66 (Oct., 1961), 757–64.

> Extract printed in *Historismus und bildende Kunst*. Munich, 1965. pp. 116–17.

> Comment *in* Peter Collins. *Changing Ideals in Modern Architecture, 1750–1950*. London, 1965. Epilogue, pp. 295–300.

> "History Repeats," *Architectural Association Journal*, 77 (Feb., 1962), 158–69. Illus. A discussion of Nikolaus Pevsner's "Modern Architecture and the Historian" and Reyner Banham's "The History of the Immediate Future."

"Obituary: Mario Labò," *Architectural Review*, 130 (Aug., 1961), 78. Illus.

"Schinkel's Bauakademie [in Berlin]," *Manchester Guardian*, June 1, 1961. Letter on its preservation.

"Sources of the Twentieth Century," *Architectural Review*, 129 (Feb., 1961), 134–35. Illus. On the Council of Europe exhibition in Paris.

"Why Not Harmonize the Old and New?" *Times*, July 3, 1961, Architects' supplement, p. xxii.

1962

"Bauhaus Comprehension," *Manchester Guardian*, March 14, 1962. Illus. On the exhibition at the Marlborough and New London galleries.

"Baukunst in England, ca. 1620–1720: Literatur 1945–1960," *Zeitschrift für Kunstgeschichte*, 25 (1962), 64–69. A bibliography.

"Faith and Feasibility: Nikolaus Pevsner Analyses the Architecture of Coventry Cathedral," *Manchester Guardian*, May 25, 1962. Illus. Plan.

"A Farewell to the Euston Propylaea," *Lodestone* (Birkbeck College, University of London), 52 (Spring, 1962), 11–12.

"Finsterlin and Some Others," *Architectural Review*, 132 (Nov., 1962), 353–57. Illus. On Hermann Finsterlin.

"Gordon Russell and Twentieth-Century Furniture," * *ibid.*, Dec., pp. 421–28. Illus.

"Jacques Groag (1892–1962)," *ibid.*, 131 (June, 1962), 380. Illus. Obituary.

"Die Kokoschka-Ausstellung in London," *Schweizer Monatshefte*, 42 (Nov., 1962), 873–76.

"Mackmurdianum," *Architectural Review*, 132 (July, 1962), 59–60. A letter by A. H. Mackmurdo to Nikolaus Pevsner, Jan. 1, 1941.

"Mendelsohn by Himself," *ibid.*, 131 (March, 1962), 161–63. Illus. With special reference to Erich Mendelsohn, *Briefe eines Architekten*.

Reprinted in *Kokusai Kentiku*, 29 (June, 1962), 20–26. Illus.

"The Perfect Suburb," *Times*, Jan. 17, Oct. 30, 1962. Letters by Nikolaus Pevsner and others on Hampstead Garden Suburb.

"Preserving Our Historic Buildings," *Simon van der Stel Foundation Bulletin*, no. 4 (April, 1962), 9–12.

"Topography: Wiltshire Surprises," *Architectural Review*, 132 (Nov., 1962), 365–67. Illus. With photographs by Eric de Maré.

1963

"Achievements in British Post-War Architecture," *Building, Lighting, Engineering* (Australia), Nov., 1963, pp. 40–41, 48.

"Architecture in Britain Today," *South African Architectural Record*, 48 (Aug., 1963), 21–22. Illus.

"Architecture in the Modern Commonwealth," *Commonwealth Journal* (Royal Commonwealth Society), Feb., 1963, pp. 21–25. Illus.

"Gropius and Van de Velde," *Architectural Review*, 133 (March, 1963), 165–68. Illus. With special reference to Henry Van de Velde, *Geschichte meines Lebens* (1962).

Letter by Walter Gropius, *ibid.*, 134 (July, 1963), 6.

"In Praise of Morris," *New Statesman*, March 22, 1963, p. 423. Letter on William Morris, in reply to an article by Reyner Banham in *ibid.*

[Letter by Nikolaus Pevsner and others on redevelopment of the Foreign Office building], *Times*, Dec. 9, 1963.

"Si ritorna all'architettura di facciata?" *Architettura*, 9 (Oct., 1963), 482–83.

* Reprinted in *Studies in Art, Architecture, and Design*, 1968.

"Skidmoring around New York," *Listener*, Aug. 22, 1963, pp. 269–71. Illus. On buildings by Skidmore, Owings, and Merrill, and others.

"Unwin Centenary," *Architectural Review*, 134 (Sept., 1963), 207–8. Illus. On Sir Raymond Unwin and his *Town Planning in Practice* (1909).

"What (and Who) Influences Quality?" *Journal of the American Institute of Architects*, 40 (July, 1963), 57–61. Address given at the 1963 Convention of the American Institute of Architects: "The Quest for Quality."

1964

"Mannerism and Elizabethan Architecture," *Listener*, Feb. 27, 1964, pp. 350–52; March 5, pp. 388–89; March 19, pp. 461–63. Illus.

"New Scotland Yard," *Architects' Journal*, June 17, 1964, p. 1333. Letter on Norman Shaw's Scotland Yard and Sir Leslie Martin's plans for Whitehall.

"Obituary: Harold Falkner, 1875–1963," *Architectural Review*, 135 (April, 1964), 240. Illus.

"The Planes in Spain," *Architects' Journal*, May 27, 1964, pp. 1176–77. Letter supporting Oriol Bohigas's protest against the unnecessary felling of trees.

With Enid Ratcliffe. "Randall Wells," *Architectural Review*, 136 (Nov., 1964), 366–68. Illus.

Letter by F. C. Keel, *ibid.*, 137 (March, 1965), 176–77.

"The Victorian Age of Building Revalued," *Times*, June 2, 1964.

1965

"Eight Paintings—A Close Analysis by Nikolaus Pevsner," *Granta*, 70 (Summer, 1965), 20–25. Illus. On paintings in the Fitzwilliam Museum, Cambridge.

"Goodhart-Rendel's Roll-Call," *Architectural Review*, 138 (Oct., 1965), 259–64. Illus. A transcript of a conversation between H. S. Goodhart-Rendel and Nikolaus Pevsner in July, 1946.

"The Preservation of the Monuments of Victorian Commerce," *Journal of Industrial Archaeology*, 2 (March, 1965), 2. Illus.

"Preserving Church Buildings," *Times*, March 10, 1965. Letter about the lack of legislation on the preservation of Roman Catholic and other churches.

"The Watchers and the Watched," *Manchester Guardian,* Jan. 29, 1965. On the exemption of Church property from planning and preservation legislation.

1966

"Architectural Bibliographers," *Architectural Review,* 140 (Oct., 1966), 237. A note on the American Association of Architectural Bibliographers.

"Architecture in Our Time: Nikolaus Pevsner on the Anti-Pioneers," *Listener,* Dec. 29, 1966, pp. 953–55; Jan. 5, 1967, pp. 7–9. Illus.

> Letters by James Stirling and Brian Roberts, *ibid.,* Jan. 12, 1967, p. 58.

> Letters by J. H. V. Davies, Gordon Rushman, Hans Unger, *ibid.,* Jan. 19, p. 97.

> Reply by Nikolaus Pevsner, *ibid.,* Feb. 2, p. 169.

> Extracts reprinted as "The Anti-Pioneers: Extracts from Two Talks on the BBC Third Programme with a Linking Summary of Professor Pevsner's Ideas on Modern Architecture and Where It Has Gone Wrong," *Architects' Journal,* Feb. 1, 1967, pp. 279–80.

>> REVIEWS:
>> *Architects' Journal,* Feb. 1, 1967, pp. 269–70. ("Waiting for the Millennium." [Editorial comment on "The Anti-Pioneers."])
>> *Architettura: cronache e storia,* 12 (April, 1967), 772–73. (Bruno Zevi. "Nikolaus Pevsner denuncia gli anti-pioneers.")

"Cityscape: Only East Germany Rivals D.C. in Paralysis of Architecture," *Washington Post,* Jan. 16, 1966.

"Edoardo Persico," *Architectural Review,* 139 (Feb., 1966), 97–98.

"Hereford Screen," *Times,* March 2, 1966. Letter on the removal of the Gilbert Scott screen from Hereford Cathedral.

"Impression of Hungarian Building," *New Hungarian Quarterly,* 7 (Spring, 1966), 46–51. Illus.

"News from Split," *Listener,* March 31, 1966, pp. 476–77.

"St. Pancras Station Must Be Saved," *Manchester Guardian,* Sept. 1, 1966. Letter.

"Zagreb," *Architectural Review,* 140 (Dec., 1966), 455–58. Illus.

1967

"Address Given by Nikolaus Pevsner at the Inauguration of the New Art and Architecture Building of Yale University, Nov. 9, 1963," *Journal of the Society of Architectural Historians*, 26 (March, 1967), 4–7. Illus.

> German tr.: "Rede zur Eröffnung des Gebäudes der Kunst- und Architekturabteilung der Universität Yale, New Haven, 9 Nov. 1963," *Bauen + Wohnen*, 19 (Nov., 1964), 432–34. Illus. Plans.

"Alahan, Better Known as Kodja Kalesi," *Architectural Review*, 141 (March, 1967), 195–97. Illus.

> Letter by J. B. Gnosspelius, *ibid.*, 142 (Aug., 1967), 83–84.

"As I See It: Morris and the Victorian," *Building Materials*, 27 (March, 1967), 13. On the William Morris Society and the Victorian Society.

"Byzantine in Herefordshire," *Country Life*, 142 (Sept. 21, 1967), 672. Letter on the condition of J. P. Seddon's church at Hoarwithy.

"Crash Course: Art in Britain," *Observer*, Feb. 10, 1967, color suppl., p. 37. A short reading list.

"Cumberland Sculptor," *Architectural Review*, 141 (June, 1967), 466. Illus. On Musgrave Lewthwaite Watson.

"L'Inghilterra e il Manierismo," *Bollettino del Centro Internazionale di Studi di Architettura Andrea Palladio*, 9 (1967), 293–303. Illus.

"Kara Dag and Alahan," *Listener*, April 6, 1967. Illus.

"Nikolaus Pevsner, 1967 Gold Medallist," *Journal of the Royal Institute of British Architects*, 3rd ser., 74 (Aug., 1967), 316–18. Port. The Royal Institute of British Architects Gold Medal address, June 20, 1967: "What Can the Architectural Historian Give to the Architect?"

> Summary reprinted as "RIBA: Sparkling Gold Medal," *Architects' Journal*, June 28, 1967, pp. 1525–26. Also includes summary of speech by Richard Sheppard.

"Palladio e il Manierismo," *Bolletino del Centro Internazionale di Studi Architettura Andrea Palladio*, 9 (1967), 304–9. Illus.

"Pevsner in the Car Pocket," *Bookseller*, Jan. 28, 1967, pp. 240–44. On writing The Buildings of England series.

"Preserving Pugin," *Times*, May 17, July 7, 1967. Letter on the screen by Pugin in the Roman Catholic cathedral in Birmingham.

"Quarr and Bellot," *Architectural Review*, 141 (April, 1967), 307–10. Illus. On Quarr Abbey, Isle of Wight, designed by Dom Paul Bellot.

"Reconstructing the Abbey," *Times,* Feb. 3, 1967. Letter on the removal of timber roofs in Westminster Abbey.

Reply by the Dean of Westminster, *ibid.* Feb. 11; reply by Nikolaus Pevsner, Feb. 16; reply by the Surveyor of the Fabric of Westminster Abbey, Feb. 18; reply by Pevsner, Feb. 28.

"Sara Losh's Church," *Architectural Review,* 142 (July, 1967), 65–67. Illus. At Wreay, Cumberland.

"University of the Ruhr," *ibid.,* Sept., pp. 233–35. Illus. Plan.

"Zehn Jahre Bauen in Grossbritannien, 1924–1934," *Bauen + Wohnen,* 22 (Dec., 1967), 461–63. Illus.

1968

"The Architectural Setting of Jane Austen's Novels," *Journal of the Warburg and Courtauld Institutes,* 31 (1968), 404–22. Illus. Maps.

"A Hungarian Exhibition in London: Hungarian Art Treasures," *New Hungarian Quarterly,* 9 (Spring, 1968), 66–68. Exhibition at the Victoria and Albert Museum.

[Letter on art education.], *Times,* July 12, 1968.

[Letter on the recording and preservation of Scottish buildings], *ibid.,* Feb. 19.

"Nikolaus Pevsner on Charles Rennie Mackintosh," *Listener,* July 4, 1968, p. 10. Extract from a broadcast centenary tribute.

"William Whewell and His Architectural Notes on German Churches," *German Life and Letters,* n.s., 22 (Oct., 1968), 38–47.

"Wotton Centenary," *Architectural Review,* 143 (June, 1968), 409. Note on Sir Henry Wotton, *Elements of Architecture* (1624).

1969

"Gropius and the Thread of History," *Casabella,* 338 (1969), 2–4.

"Hyperbolic Towers," *Architectural Review,* 145 (April, 1969), 298. On the design of hyperbolic cooling towers.

[Letter on Professor R. Branner's review, *Art Bulletin,* 50 (1968), 199, of Paul Frankl, *Gothic Architecture* (Pelican History of Art)], *Art Bulletin,* 51 (March, 1969), 101.

[Letter on review in *Times Literary Supplement,* May 15, 1969, of *Concern-*

72　　　　　　　　　　　　　　　　　　　　SIR NIKOLAUS PEVSNER

ing Architecture: Essays on Architectural Writers and Writing Presented to Nikolaus Pevsner (London, 1968)], *Times Literary Supplement*, May 29, 1969.

"Reynolds's *Discourses*," *Listener*, Feb. 20, 1969, pp. 234–36.

"An Unknown Albert Memorial," *Architectural Review*, 146 (Dec., 1969), 469. On drawings by J. I. Hittorf for the Albert Memorial.

BOOKS REVIEWED BY SIR NIKOLAUS PEVSNER

Addleshaw, G. W. C., and Frederick Etchells. *The Architectural Setting of Anglican Worship*. London, 1948.

> In LISTENER, Oct. 28, 1948, pp. 657–58.

Alberti, Leon Battista. *L'architettura*. Tr. by Giovanni Orlandi. Milan, 1966. Introduction and notes by Paolo Portoghesi.

> In ARCHITECTURAL REVIEW, 142 (July, 1967), 7.

Andrews, Wayne. *Architecture in Michigan*. Detroit, 1967.

> In ARCHITECTURAL REVIEW, 144 (Dec., 1968), 466.

Arslan, Wart. *I Bassano*. Bologna, 1931.

> In ZEITSCHRIFT FÜR KUNSTGESCHICHTE, 1 (1932), 163–65.

Ascione, Enrico, and Italo Insolera, eds. *Coste d'Italia dal Gargano al Tevere*. Rome, 1967.

> In ARCHITECTURAL REVIEW, 143 (May, 1968), 333.

—— and others, eds. *Coste d'Italia: la Sicilia*. Rome, 1969.

> In ARCHITECTURAL REVIEW, 146 (July, 1969), 84.

Aubert, Marcel, and Simone Goubet. *Gothic Cathedrals of France and Their Treasures [Cathédrales et trésors gothiques de France]*. London, 1959.

> In ARCHITECTURAL REVIEW, 127 (May, 1960), 299.

——. *Romanesque Cathedrals and Abbeys of France [Cathédrales, abbatiales, collégiales, prieurés romans de France]*. Tr. by Cuthbert Girdlestone. London, 1966.

> In ARCHITECTURAL REVIEW, 143 (Feb., 1968), 99.

Baker, John. *English Stained Glass*. London, 1960.

> In MANCHESTER GUARDIAN, July 15, 1960. Illus. ("Painted Miracles of the High Gothic.")

Baldass, Ludwig von. *Conrad Laib und die beiden Rueland Frueauf*. Vienna, 1946.

In Times Literary Supplement, May 22, 1948, p. 290.

Banham, Reyner. *The New Brutalism*. London, 1966.

In Manchester Guardian, Dec. 9, 1966.

Bardi, P. M. *The Arts in Brazil: A New Museum at São Paulo*. Tr. from the Italian by John Drummond. Milan, 1956.

In Times Literary Supplement, Feb. 15, 1957, p. 95.

Bell, Quentin. *The Schools of Design*. London, 1963.

In Times Literary Supplement, Nov. 1, 1963, p. 880.

Benesch, Otto. *The Art of the Renaissance in Northern Europe*. Cambridge. Mass., 1945.

In Burlington Magazine, 89 (Dec., 1947), 352.

Bertram, Anthony. *The House: A Machine for Living in*. 2nd ed. London, 1945.

In Architectural Review, 98 (Aug., 1945), 59–60.

Best, R. D. *Brass Chandelier: A Biography of R. H. Best of Birmingham*. London, 1940.

In Architectural Review, 89 (Jan., 1941), 25–26. Illus.

Blomfield, Sir Reginald. *Richard Norman Shaw, 1831–1912*. London, 1940.

In Architectural Review, 89 (Jan., 1941), 41–46. Illus.

Reprinted in Peter Ferriday, ed. *Victorian Architecture*. 1963;

In Burlington Magazine, 78 (June, 1941), 202–3.

Blunt, Anthony. *Philibert de l'Orme*. London, 1958. (Studies in Architecture, no. 1.)

In Times Literary Supplement, May, 9, 1958, pp. 249–50.

Boase, T. S. R. *English Art, 1800–1870*. Oxford, 1959. (Oxford History of English Art, vol. 10.)

In Listener, July 23, 1959, p. 142.

Bodkin, Thomas. *Dismembered Masterpieces: A Plea for Their Reconstruction by International Action*. London, 1945.

In Spectator, March 30, 1945, p. 293.

——, ed. *The Paintings of Jan Vermeer*. London, 1940. With an introduction by Thomas Bodkin.

In Spectator, May 16, 1941, p. 532.

Boeck, Wilhelm. *Der Bamberger Meister*. Tübingen, 1960.

In Burlington Magazine, 103 (March, 1961), 111.

Bournville Village Trust. *Sixty Years of Planning: The Bournville Experiment*. Bournville, 1942.

In ARCHITECTURAL REVIEW, 92 (Nov., 1942), 128. Illus.

Branner, Robert. *Burgundian Gothic Architecture*. London, 1960. (Studies in Architecture, no. 3.)

In ARCHITECTURAL REVIEW, 130 (Oct., 1961), 226.

Brieger, Peter. *Die deutsche Geschichtsmalerei des 19. Jahrhunderts*. Berlin, 1930. (Kunstwissenschaftliche Studien, 8.)

In BELVEDERE, 10 (Feb., 1931), 68–69.

Briggs, Asa, ed. *William Morris: Selected Writings and Designs*. Harmondsworth, 1962.

In MANCHESTER GUARDIAN, Jan. 25, 1963. ("Master Morris.")

Briggs, Martin S. *The Architect in History*. Oxford, 1927.

In KRITISCHE BERICHTE ZUR KUNSTGESCHICHTLICHEN LITERATUR, Jahrg. 3/4 (1930/32), pp. 97–122. ("Zur Geschichte des Architektenberufs.")

Britain under Fire. London, 1941. With a foreword by J. B. Priestley.

In BURLINGTON MAGAZINE, 79 (Sept., 1941), 101–2.

Bronstein, Leo. *El Greco*. London, 1951. (Library of Great Painters.)

In SPECTATOR, Nov., 1951, p. 660.

The Buildings of Yale University. New Haven, 1964.

In ARCHITECTURAL REVIEW, 142 (Nov., 1967), 331.

Bullrich, Francisco. *Arquitectura argentina contemporanea*. Buenos Aires, 1964.

In ARCHITECTURAL REVIEW, 137 (April, 1965), 255.

Bund Deutscher Architekten [and others]. *Planen und Bauen im neuen Deutschland*. Cologne and Opladen, 1960.

In ARCHITECTURAL REVIEW, 130 (Sept., 1961), 152.

Bunim, Miriam S. *Space in Medieval Painting and the Forerunners of Perspective*. New York, 1940.

In BURLINGTON MAGAZINE, 81 (Dec., 1942), 311.

Bunting, Bainbridge. *Houses of Boston's Back Bay*. Cambridge, Mass., 1968.

In ARCHITECTURAL REVIEW, 144 (July, 1968), 72.

Burke, Thomas. *The Streets of London through the Centuries*. London, 1940.

In SPECTATOR, Jan. 24, 1941, pp. 93–94.

Burnett, R. G. *Oxford and Cambridge in Pictures: Photography by E. W. Tattersall*. London, 1950.

In CAMBRIDGE REVIEW, Oct. 21, 1950, p. 52.

Butler, Arthur S. G. *The Architecture of Sir Edwin Lutyens,* London, New York, 1950. (Lutyens memorial volumes.)

> In ARCHITECTURAL REVIEW, 109 (April, 1951), 217–25. Illus. ("Building with Wit.")

Byng-Stamper, Frances, and C. Lucas. *Twelfth Century Paintings at Hardham and Clayton.* Lewes, 1947. Photographs by Helmut Gernsheim.

> In ARCHITECTURAL REVIEW, 102 (Dec., 1947), 208.

Camón Aznar, José. *La arquitectura plateresca.* Consejo Superior de Investigaciones Cientificas, Instituto Diego Velasquez: Madrid, 1945.

> In BURLINGTON MAGAZINE, 90 (Jan., 1948), 24.

Carter, Ernestine, ed. *Grim Glory: Pictures of Britain under Fire.* London, 1941.

> In BURLINGTON MAGAZINE, 79 (Sept., 1941), 101–2.

Casey, Maie, ed. *Early Melbourne Architecture: 1840–1888.* 2nd ed. Melbourne and New York, 1965.

> In ARCHITECTURAL REVIEW, 137 (Jan., 1965), 7. Illus.

Catalogue of Printers and Draughtsmen Represented in the Library of Reproductions of Pictures and Drawings formed by Sir Robert and Lady Witt. London, 1920, 1925.

> In ZEITSCHRIFT FÜR BILDENDE KUNST, 60, *Kunstchronik,* Feb., 1927, pp. 130–31.

Cave, C. J. P. *Roof Bosses in Mediaeval Churches.* Cambridge, 1948.

> In ARCHITECTURAL REVIEW, 107 (April, 1950), 276.

Chambers's Encyclopedia. New edition. London, 1950.

> In ARCHITECTURAL REVIEW, 109 (Feb., 1951), 121–22.

Chase, Isabel W. U. *Horace Walpole, Gardenist: An Edition of Walpole's "The History of Modern Taste in Gardening."* Princeton, 1943.

> In ARCHITECTURAL REVIEW, 95 (Feb., 1944), 56. [Signed Peter F. R. Donner, i.e., Nikolaus Pevsner.]

Chiolini, Paolo. *I caratteri distributivi degli antichi edifici, gli edifici romani, gli edifici del medio evo.* Milan, 1959.

> In ARCHITECTURAL REVIEW, 127 (Jan., 1960), 5.

Christ, Yvan. *Projets et divagations de Claude-Nicolas Ledoux, architecte du roi.* Paris, 1961.

> In TIMES LITERARY SUPPLEMENT, Jan. 12, 1962, p. 20.

Clark, Sir Kenneth. *Landscape into Art.* London, 1949.

> In ARCHITECTURAL REVIEW, 108 (Aug., 1950), 133–34.

Clark, Sir Kenneth. *Ruskin Today*. London, 1964.

>In Manchester Guardian, Nov. 27, 1964. ("The Perverseness of Ruskin.")

Clarke, Basil F. L. *Anglican Cathedrals outside the British Isles*. London, 1958.

>In Times Literary Supplement, June 26, 1959, p. 380.

——. *The Building of the Eighteenth Century Church*. London, 1963.

>In Architectural Review, 136 (Sept., 1964), 163.

Clasen, Karl Heinz. *Deutsche Gewölbe der Spätgotik*. Berlin, 1958. (Deutsche Bauakademie. Schriften.)

>In Art Bulletin, 41 (1959), 333–36. Illus.

Clawson, H. Phelps. *"By Their Works," Illustrated from the Collections in the Buffalo Museum of Science*. Buffalo, N.Y., 1941.

>In Burlington Magazine, 81 (Nov., 1942), 286.

Collins, Peter. *Changing Ideals in Modern Architecture, 1750–1950*. London, 1965.

>In Manchester Guardian, May 28, 1965.

Cook, G. H. *English Collegiate Churches of the Middle Ages*. London, 1959.

>In Listener, Dec. 3, 1959, pp. 994–95.

——. *English Monasteries in the Middle Ages*. London, 1961.

>In Manchester Guardian, Nov. 24, 1961. ("The English Monastery.")

——. *Portrait of Durham Cathedral*. London, 1948.

>In Architectural Review, 105 (April, 1949), 198–99.

Coolidge, John R. *Mill and Mansion: A Study of Architecture and Society in Lowell, Mass., 1820–1865*. New York, 1942. (Columbia Studies in American Culture, no. 10.)

>In Architectural Review, 94 (July, 1943), 26–28.

Cox-Johnson, Ann. *John Bacon, R.A., 1740–1799*. London, 1961. (St. Marylebone Society Publication, no. 4.)

>In Journal of the Royal Society of Arts, 110 (April, 1962), 355–56.

Crossley, Frederick H. *English Church Craftsmanship*. London, 1941. (British Heritage Series.)

>In Architectural Review, 90 (Dec., 1941), 182. [Signed by Peter F. R. Donner, i.e., Nikolaus Pevsner.]

Curman, Sigurd, and Johnny Roosval, eds. *Sveriges Kyrkor: Konsthistoriskt*

Inventarium. Uppland. Vol. 7, **pt.** 1: *Bro Härad.* By Armin Tuulse. Stockholm, 1956.

In Times Literary Supplement, March 8, 1957, p. 148.

Curran, Charles P. *The Rotunda Hospital: Its Architects and Craftsmen.* Dublin, 1945.

In Architectural Review, 102 (Nov., 1947), 176.

Damerini, Gino. *I pittori veneziani del Settecento.* Bologna, 1928.

In Göttingische gelehrte Anzeigen, 191 (Oct., 1929), 417–39. Plate. Bibliog.

Denucé, J. *Kunstausfuhr Antwerpens im 17. Jahrhundert: Die Firma Forschoudt.* Antwerp, 1931. (Quellen zur Geschichte der flämischen Kunst, Bd. 1.)

In Deutsche Literaturzeitung, May 1, 1932, pp. 844–45.

De Vito Battaglia, Silvia. *Correggio: Bibliografia.* Rome, 1934. (Reale Istituto di archeologia e storia dell'arte. Bibliografie e cataloghi, vol. 3.)

In Göttingische gelehrte Anzeigen, 197 (Dec., 1935), 499–504.

Dickinson, J. C. *Monastic Life in Mediaeval England.* London, 1961.

In Manchester Guardian, Nov. 24, 1961. ("The English Monastery.")

Dmochowski, Zbigniew. *The Architecture of Poland: An Historical Survey.* London, 1956.

In Times Literary Supplement, June 7, 1957, p. 352.

Downes, Kerry. *Hawksmoor.* London, 1959. (Studies in Architecture, no. 2.)

In Listener, Dec. 31, 1959, p. 1166.

Dutton, Ralph. *The Age of Wren.* London, 1951.

In Cambridge Review, May 24, 1952, p. 517.

Effmann, Wilhelm. *Zur Baugeschichte des Hildesheimer Domes.* Hildesheim and Leipzig, 1933. (Der Hildesheimer Dom, Bd. 1.)

In Die Denkmalpflege, 1933, pp. 210–14.

Esdaile, Katherine A. *English Church Monuments, 1510 to 1840.* London, 1947.

In Times Literary Supplement, Aug. 9, 1947, pp. 397–98.

———. *St. Martin in the Fields, New and Old.* London, 1944.

In Architectural Review, 97 (Jan., 1945), 32.

Evans, Joan. *Art in Mediaeval France, 937–1498.* London, 1948.

In Architectural Review, 106 (Nov., 1949), 334.

Evans, Joan. *English Art. 1307–1461.* Oxford, 1949. (Oxford History of English Art, vol. 5.)

  In Times Literary Supplement, Jan. 13, 1950, pp. 17–18.

——. *Monastic Architecture in France from the Renaissance to the Revolution.* Cambridge, 1964.

  In Architectural Review, 136 (Oct., 1964), 241.

Faczynski, Jerzy. *Studies in Polish Architecture.* Liverpool, London, 1945.

  In Architectural Review, 98 (Nov., 1945), 148. [Signed Peter F. R. Donner, i.e., Nikolaus Pevsner.]

Fanelli, Giovanni. *Architettura moderna in Olanda.* Florence, 1968.

  In Architectural Review, 145 (April, 1969), 308.

Fehr, Götz. *Benedikt Ried.* Munich, 1961.

  In Architectural Review, 131 (April, 1962), 232. Illus.

Felton, Herbert, and John Harvey. *The English Cathedrals.* London, 1950.

  In Architectural Review, 110 (July, 1951), 59–60.

Fiocco, Giuseppe. *Die venezianische Malerei des 17. u. 18. Jahrhunderts.* Florence, Munich, 1929.

  In Repertorium für Kunstwissenschaft, 51 (1930), 263–65.

Fisher, Ernest A. *Greater Anglo-Saxon Churches: An Architectural Historical Study.* London, 1962.

  In Times Literary Supplement, Aug. 9, 1963, p. 604.

Fitchen, John. *The Construction of Gothic Cathedrals: A Study of Medieval Vault Erection.* Oxford, 1961.

  In Architectural Review, 129 (May, 1961), 298–99.

Fleming, John. *Robert Adam and His Circle in Edinburgh and Rome.* London, 1962.

  In Listener, March 8, 1962, p. 427.

Forssman, Erik. *Palladio's Lehrgebäude.* Stockholm, 1965. (Acta Universitatis Stockholmiensis, vol. 9.)

  In Architectural Review, 138 (July, 1965), 7.

Freeland, John M. *Melbourne Churches, 1836–51: An Architectural Record.* Melbourne, 1963.

  In Architectural Review, 137 (Jan. 1965), 7.

Fürst, Viktor. *The Architecture of Sir Christopher Wren.* London, 1956.

  In Times Literary Supplement, June 15, 1956, pp. 353–54.

Garas, Klára. *Franz Anton Maulbertsch, 1724–96.* Budapest, 1960.

  In Times Literary Supplement, April 19, 1960, p. 260.

Gardner, Alfred H. *Outline of English Architecture.* London, 1945.
    In ARCHITECTURAL REVIEW, 99 (May, 1946), 156.
Gardner, Arthur. *English Medieval Sculpture.* Cambridge, 1951.
    In CAMBRIDGE REVIEW, Nov. 17, 1951, p. 136.
Gaudí. Barcelona, 1959. Preface by Le Corbusier.
    In ARCHITECTURAL REVIEW, 127 (May, 1960), 299.
Gaunt, William. *London.* London, 1961.
    In LISTENER, Jan. 11, 1962, p. 81.
Geretsegger, Heinz, and Max Peinter. *Otto Wagner, 1841–1918.* Salzburg, 1964.
    In TIMES LITERARY SUPPLEMENT, Feb. 18, 1965, p. 129.
Giedion, Sigfried. *Mechanization Takes Command: A Contribution to Anonymous History.* New York, 1948. ("Judges VI, 34: But the Spirit of the Lord Came upon Gideon and He Blew a Trumpet.")
    In ARCHITECTURAL REVIEW, 106 (Aug., 1949), 77–79.
    In TIMES LITERARY SUPPLEMENT, Oct. 28, 1949, p. 700.
——. *Space, Time, and Architecture: The Growth of a New Tradition.* Cambridge, Mass., London, 1941. (Charles Eliot Norton lectures, 1938–39.)
    In BURLINGTON MAGAZINE, 82 (Jan., 1943), 25–26.
Gloag, John. *English Furniture.* 2nd ed. London, 1944. (Library of English Art.)
    In ARCHITECTURAL REVIEW, 99 (Feb., 1946), 64.
——. *Industrial Art Explained.* Rev. and enl. ed. London, 1946.
    In ARCHITECTURAL REVIEW, 101 (Feb., 1947), 71–72.
——, and Derek Bridgwater. *A History of Cast Iron in Architecture.* London, 1948.
    In TIMES LITERARY SUPPLEMENT, Jan. 15, 1949, p. 42.
Gombrich, Ernst H. *The Story of Art.* London, 1949.
    In LISTENER, Dec. 8, 1949, p. 1018. Illus.
Goodhart-Rendel, H. S. *English Architecture since the Regency.* London, 1953.
    In ARCHITECTURAL REVIEW, 115 (June, 1954), 367–69. ("Originality.")
    Letter by H. S. Goodhart-Rendel, *ibid.*, 116 (Sept., 1954), 142.
Götz, Wolfgang. *Zentralbau und Zentralbauten in der gotischen Architektur.* Berlin, 1968.
    In ARCHITECTURAL REVIEW, 145 (April, 1969), 308.

Grisebach, August. *Römische Porträtbüsten der Gegenreformation.* Leipzig, 1936. (Römische Forschungen der Bibliotheca Hertziana, Bd. 13.)

    In GÖTTINGISCHE GELEHRTE ANZEIGEN, 199, no. 2/3 (1937), 92–95.

Grivot, Denis, and George Zarnecki. *Gislebertus: Sculptor of Autun.* Paris, London, 1961.

    In ARCHITECTURAL REVIEW, 131 (Feb., 1962), 85. Illus.

Gropius, Walter, and S. P. Harkness, eds. *Twenty Years of TAC* [i.e., The Architects' Collaborative, 1945–65]. Teufen, 1966.

    In ARCHITECTURAL REVIEW, 140 (Dec., 1966), 397.

Gurlitt, Hildebrand, ed. *Peter Paul Rubens: Genua. Palazzi di Genova, 1622.* Berlin, 1924. (Bibliothek alter Meister der Baukunst, Bd. 3.)

    In DER CICERONE, 19 (1927), 27.

Gwynn, Denis. *Lord Shrewsbury, Pugin and the Catholic Revival.* London, 1946.

    In ARCHITECTURAL REVIEW, 101 (June, 1947), 228. [Signed by Peter F. R. Donner, i.e., Nikolaus Pevsner.]

Habicht, Victor Curt. *Niedersächsische Kunst in England.* Hanover, 1930. (Schriftenreihe der wirtschaftwissenschaftlichen Gesellschaft zum Studium Niedersachsens.)

    In ZEITSCHRIFT FÜR BILDENDE KUNST, 65, "Kunstchronik," Aug.– Sept., 1931, p. 55.

Hamlin, Talbot F. *Architecture, an Art for All Men.* New York, London, 1947.

    In BURLINGTON MAGAZINE, March 1948, pp. 86–87.

——. *Greek Revival Architecture in America.* New York, 1944.

    In BURLINGTON MAGAZINE, 86 (June, 1945), 153–54.

Harvey, John H. *English Mediaeval Architects: A Biographical Dictionary down to 1550.* London, 1954.

    In ARCHITECTURAL REVIEW, 118 (Oct., 1955), 259–60.

    Letter by J. H. Harvey, *ibid.,* 119 (Jan., 1956), 2.

——. *Gothic England.* London, 1947.

    In LISTENER, Sept. 11, 1947, pp. 440–41. Illus.

——. *The Gothic World, 1100–1600: A Survey of Architecture and Art.* London, 1950.

    In CAMBRIDGE REVIEW, Jan. 27, 1951, 282–84.

Harwood, A. C., ed. *The Faithful Thinker: Centenary Essays on the Work and Thought of Rudolf Steiner, 1861–1925.* London, 1961.

In ARCHITECTURAL REVIEW, 130 (Sept., 1961), 153.

Hauser, Arnold. *The Social History of Art.* London, 1951.

In TIMES LITERARY SUPPLEMENT, Dec. 28, 1951, pp. 829–30.

Hederer, Oswald. *Leo von Klenze: Persönlichkeit und Werk.* Munich, 1964.

In TIMES LITERARY SUPPLEMENT, July 9, 1964, p. 584.

Henderson, Philip. *William Morris: His Life, Work, and Friends.* London, 1968.

In ARCHITECTURAL REVIEW, 144 (Oct., 1968), 287–88 ("Triple Morris.")

Hennig-Schefold, N., and I. Schaefer. *Frühe Moderne in Berlin.* Winterthur, 1967.

In ARCHITECTURAL REVIEW, 143 (March, 1968), 177.

Henry Moore: Sculpture and Drawings. London, 1944. Intro. by Herbert Read.

In BURLINGTON MAGAZINE, 86 (Feb., 1945), 47–49.

Hess, Jacob. *Agostino Tassi, der Lehrer des Claude Lorrain: Ein Beitrag zur Geschichte der Barockmalerei in Rom.* Munich, 1935.

In ART BULLETIN, 17 (Dec., 1935), 511.

Hill, Sir George. *The Medal: Its Place in Art. Annual Lecture on Aspects of Art, Henriette Hertz Trust of the British Academy.* London, 1941.

In BURLINGTON MAGAZINE, 82 (June, 1943), 156.

Hirschfeld, Werner. *Das Zisterzienserkloster Pforte, Geschichte seiner romanischen Bauten.* Burg bei Magdeburg, 1933. (Beiträge zur Kunstgeschichte, Bd. 2.)

In DEUTSCHE KUNST UND DENKMALPFLEGE, 1934, pt. 5–6, pp. 134–35.

Hitchcock, Henry-Russell. *Early Victorian Architecture in Britain.* New Haven, London, 1954.

In ANTIQUARIES' JOURNAL, 36 (Jan.-April, 1956), 133–35.

In TIMES LITERARY SUPPLEMENT, June 3, 1955, p. 300.

Hoffmann, H. C. *Die Theaterbauten von Fellner und Helmer.* Munich, 1966. (Forschungsunternehmen der Fritz Thyssen Stiftung, Arbeitskreis Kunstgeschichte. Studien zur Kunst des neunzehnten Jahrhunderts, Bd. 2.)

In ARCHITECTURAL REVIEW, 143 (Jan., 1968), 7. Illus. Plan.

Hoffmann, Hans. *Hochrenaissance, Manierismus, Frühbarock: Die italienische Kunst des 16. Jahrhunderts.* Zurich and Leipzig, 1939.

In BURLINGTON MAGAZINE, 75 (Sept., 1939), 136.

Holst, Niels von. *Künstler, Sammler, Publikum.* Neuwied am Rhein and Berlin-Spandau, 1961.

In Times Literary Supplement, Dec. 8, 1961, p. 880.

Homburger, Otto. *Museumkunde.* Breslau, 1924.

In Der Cicerone, 17 (1925), 963–64.

Howarth, Thomas. *Charles Rennie Mackintosh and the Modern Movement.* London, 1952. (Glasgow University Publications, no. 94.)

In Burlington Magazine, 95 (Sept., 1953), 311.

Hürlimann, Martin, and Jean Bony. *French Cathedrals.* London, 1951.

In Architectural Review, 112 (Nov., 1952), 335.

——, and Peter Meyer. *English Cathedrals.* London, 1950.

In Architectural Review, 110 (July, 1951), 59–60.

Hussey, Christopher. *Life of Sir Edwin Lutyens.* London, New York, 1950. (Lutyens memorial volumes.)

In Architectural Review, 109 (April, 1951), 217–25. Illus. ("Building with Wit.")

Joedicke, Jürgen. *A History of Modern Architecture. [Geschichte der modernen Architektur].* Tr. by James C. Palmes. London, 1959.

In Architectural Review, 127 (Feb., 1960), 81.

Jones, Sydney. *London Triumphant.* London, New York, 1942.

In Architectural Review, 92 (Oct., 1942), 103–4.

Kimball, Sidney Fiske. *The Creation of the Rococo.* Philadelphia, 1943.

In Times Literary Supplement, March 23, 1946, pp. 133–34.

Kindlers Malereilexikon. Bd. 1, A-C. Zurich, 1964.

In Times Literary Supplement, Sept. 30, 1965, p. 869.

Kultermann, Udo, ed. *Die gläserne Kette: Visionäre Architekturen aus dem Kreis um Bruno Taut, 1919–20.* Leverkusen, 1963. Exhibition in the Leverkusen Museum, 1963.

In Architectural Review, 135 (April, 1964), 241. Illus.

——. *Neues Bauen in der Welt.* Tübingen, 1965.

In Architectural Review, 140 (July, 1966), 7.

Die Kunstdenkmäler der Schweiz. Vols. 3, 7, 8. Basel, 1948.

In Burlington Magazine, 90 (Aug., 1948), 242; 91 (Sept., 1949), 266; (Nov., 1949), 299. The publications of the Gesellschaft für Schweizerische Altertumskunde are compared with those of the Royal Commission on Historic Monuments.

Labò, Mario. *Architettura e arredamento del negozio.* Milan, 1936.

In Architectural Review, 83 (June, 1938), 311–12.

Lancaster, Osbert. *Häuser machen Leute* [*Here of All Places*]. Tr. by E. T. Kauer and U. von Puttkamer. Berlin, 1960.

In Journal of the Royal Institute of British Architects, 3rd ser., 68 (July, 1961), 369.

Lang, Ludwig. *Was ist Barock?* Zürich and Stuttgart, 1924. (Montana-Kunstführer, Bd. 1.)

In Der Cicerone, 18 (1926), 238.

Langenskiöld, Eric J. *Michele Sanmicheli, the Architect of Verona: His Life and Works.* Uppsala, 1938. (Uppsala-Studier i arkeologi och konsthistoria, 1.)

In Architectural Review, 96 (Dec., 1944), 187–88.

Langkilde, Hans. *Arkitekten Kay Fisker.* Copenhagen, 1960.

In Architectural Review, 130 (Nov., 1961), 301.

Lavedan, Pierre. *Histoire de l'urbanisme.* Vol. 2. *Renaissance et temps modernes.* Paris, 1941.

In Architectural Review, 102 (Sept., 1947), 103.

Le Corbusier. *The Modulor: A Harmonious Measure to the Human Scale Universally Applicable to Architecture and Mechanics.* Tr. by Peter de Francia and Anna Bostock. London, 1954.

In Cambridge Review, May 15, 1954, p. 456.

Lees-Milne, James. *Tudor Renaissance.* London, 1951. (British Art and Building Series.)

In Architectural Review, 112 (Oct., 1952), 261.

Lenning, Henry F. *The Art Nouveau.* The Hague, 1951.

In Architectural Review, 113 (March, 1953), 191.

Levi d'Ancona, Ezio. *Botteghe e canzoni della vecchia Firenze.* Bologna, 1927.

In Zeitschrift für bildende Kunst, 62, "Kunstchronik," Feb.–March, 1929, p. 137.

Lewis, Lesley. *Connoisseurs and Secret Agents in Eighteenth-Century Rome.* London, 1961.

In Times Literary Supplement, Dec. 8, 1961, p. 880.

Lissitzky, El. *1929 Russland: Architektur für eine Weltrevolution.* Frankfurt and Vienna, 1965. (Ullstein Bauwelt-Fundamente, 14.)

In Architectural Review, 138 (Nov., 1965), 319.

London County Council. *Survey of London.* Vol. 21. *The Parish of St. Pancras.* Pt. 3. *Tottenham Court Road and Neighbourhood.* London, 1949.

In Architectural Review, 108 (Aug., 1950), 134.

London County Council. *Survey of London.* Vol. 22. *Bankside.* London, 1950.
    In Architectural Review, 109 (April, 1951), 261–62.
Loos, Adolf. *Sämtliche Schriften.* Ed. by Franz Glück. Vienna, 1963.
    In Times Literary Supplement, Sept. 27, 1963, p. 727.
McGrath, Raymond, and A. C. Frost. *Glass in Architecture and Decoration.* London, 1937.
    In Architectural Review, 83 (Jan., 1938), 42–43.
Madsen, Stefan Tschudi. *Sources of Art Nouveau.* Oslo, 1956.
    In Architectural Review, 122 (Nov., 1957), 297–99. Illus. ("Beautiful, and If Need Be, Useful.")
    Letter by Geoffrey Newman, *ibid.,* 124 (Nov., 1958), 282. ("Art Nouveau.")
Magnuson, Torgil. *Studies in Roman Quattrocento Architecture.* Stockholm, 1958. (Figura, 9.)
    In Architectural Review, 125 (April, 1959), 288.
Mariani, Valerio. *Mattia Preti a Malta.* Rome, 1929.
    In Belvedere, 8 (Dec., 1929), 461–63.
Martin, John Rupert. *The Farnese Gallery.* Princeton, 1965. (Princeton Monograph on Art and Archaeology, no. 36.)
    In Times Literary Supplement, Sept. 9, 1965, p. 770.
Meiss, Millard, ed. *Essays in Honor of Erwin Panofsky.* New York, 1961. (De artibus opuscula, 40.)
    In Times Literary Supplement, June 28, 1961, p. 460.
Mendelsohn, Erich. *Briefe eines Architekten.* Munich, 1961.
    In Architectural Review, 131 (March, 1962), 160–63. Reprinted in *Kokusai Kentiku,* 29 (June, 1962), 20–26. Illus. See also Nikolaus Pevsner's introduction to the English translation, 1967.
Meyer, Peter. *Europäische Kunstgeschichte.* Pt. 1. Zürich, 1947.
    In Architectural Review, 105 (Feb., 1949), 96.
Michalski, Ernst. *Die Bedeutung der ästhetischen Grenze für die Methode der Kunstgeschichte.* Berlin, 1932. (Kunstwissenschaftliche Studien, Bd. 11.)
    In Zeitschrift für Kunstgeschichte, 2 (1933), 40–44.
Michele Sanmicheli: Studi raccolti dall' Accademia di Agricoltura, Scienze e Lettere di Verona per la celebrazione del IV centenario della morte. Verona, 1960.
    In Times Literary Supplement, April 6, 1962, p. 228.
Mindlin, Henrique E. *Modern Architecture in Brazil.* London, 1956.

In Times Literary Supplement, Feb. 15, 1957, p. 95.

Möbius, Helga, and Friedrich Möbius. *Mediaeval Churches in Germany*. London, 1965.

In Architectural Review, 139 (May, 1966), 327.

Mock, Elizabeth B., ed. *Built in U.S.A., 1932–1944*. New York, 1944.

In Burlington Magazine, 86 (Nov., 1945), 285–86.

Moore, Henry. *Shelter Sketch Book*. London, 1945.

In Architectural Review, 98 (Nov., 1945), 147.

Morrell, John B. *The Biography of the Common Man of the City of York as Recorded in His Epitaph*. London, 1947.

In Architectural Review, 104 (April, 1948), 172. [Signed by Peter F. R. Donner, i.e., Nikolaus Pevsner.]

——. *York Monuments*. London, 1944. (The Arts and Crafts in York.)

In Architectural Review, 97 (May, 1945), 156.

Müller, E. [and others]. *Leipziger Bautradition*. Leipzig, 1955.

In Architectural Review, 119 (Feb., 1956), 132.

Mumford, Lewis. *Art and Technics*. New York, 1952.

In Magazine of Art, 45 (Dec., 1952), 379.

Munnings, Sir Alfred. *An Artist's Life: An Autobiography*. London, 1950–52.

In Cambridge Review, Jan. 20, 1951, p. 260.

Münz, Ludwig, and Gustav Künstler. *Der Architekt Adolf Loos*. Vienna, 1964.

In Times Literary Supplement, Feb. 11, 1965, p. 100.

National Gallery, London. *From the National Gallery Laboratory*. London, 1940. Photographs with notes by Ian Rawlins.

In Burlington Magazine, 80 (June, 1942), 155–56.

Nervi, Pier Luigi. *Aesthetics and Technology in Building*. Cambridge, Mass., 1966. (Charles Eliot Norton lectures, 1961–62.)

In New York Review of Books, June 3, 1966, pp. 24–25.

——. *The Works of Pier Luigi Nervi*. London, 1957.

In Architectural Review, 123 (June, 1958), 417–18.

Newton, Eric. *Tintoretto*. London, 1952.

In Architectural Review, 111 (June, 1952), 361–65. Illus. ("Tintoretto and Mannerism.")

Letter by Eric Newton, followed by a reply by Nikolaus Pevsner, *ibid.*, 112 (Sept., 1952), 203–4.

Letter by Renato Bernesthal, *ibid.*, Nov., p. 343. Illus.

Newton, Roger H. *Town and Davis, Pioneers in American Revivalist Architecture, 1812–1870.* New York, 1942. Ithiel Town, 1784–1844, and A. J. Davis, 1803–92.

In Architectural Review, 94 (July, 1943), 26–28.

Nicodemi, Giorgio. *Pier Francesco Mazzucchelli detto il Morazzone.* Varese, 1927.

In Repertorium für Kunstwissenschaft, 51 (1930), 260–63.

Nisser, Wilhelm. *Michael Dahl and the Contemporary Swedish School of Painting.* Uppsala, 1927.

In Zeitschrift für bildende Kunst, 62, "Kunstchronik," Nov., 1928, p. 97.

Ozinga, M. D. *De Monumenten van Curaçao in woord en beeld.* Amsterdam, Willemstad, 1959.

In Architectural Review, 128 (Nov., 1960), 323.

———. *De protestantsche Kerkenbouw in Nederland van Herforming tot franschen Tijd.* Amsterdam, 1938.

In Burlington Magazine, 73 (Sept., 1938), 134–35.

Pach, Walter. *Pierre Auguste Renoir.* London, 1951. (Library of Great Painters.)

In Spectator, Nov. 16, 1951, p. 660.

Palme, Per. *Triumph of Peace: A Study of the Whitehall Banqueting House.* Stockholm, 1956. (Figura, 8.)

In Times Literary Supplement, Dec. 21, 1956, p. 766.

Pane, Roberto. *Andrea Palladio.* Turin, 1961. (Collana storica di architettura, 5.)

In Architectural Review, 132 (Aug., 1962), 81. Translated in *Boletín Bibliográfico, Instituto interuniversitario de especialización en historia de la arquitectura* (Córdoba, Argentina), no. 4 (June, 1961), 46–47.

Panofsky, Erwin. *Gothic Architecture and Scholasticism.* New York, London, 1957.

In Times Literary Supplement, Jan. 24, 1958, p. 49.

———. *Tomb Sculpture: Its Changing Aspects from Ancient Egypt to Bernini.* London, 1964.

In Times Literary Supplement, Jan. 14, 1965, p. 31.

Pantin, W. A. *Durham Cathedral.* London, 1948.

In Architectural Review, 105 (April, 1949), 198–99.

Paoletti, Pietro. *La Scuola Grande di San Marco, Venezia.* Venice, 1929.

In Zeitschrift für bildende Kunst, 64, "Kunstchronik," June–July, 1930, pp. 17–18.

Paulsson, Thomas. *Scandinavian Architecture*. London, 1958.

In Times Literary Supplement, March 20, 1959, p. 163.

Persico, Edoardo. *Tutte le opere, 1923–1935*. Milan, 1964. (Saggi di cultura contemporanea, 43.)

In Architectural Review, 139 (Feb., 1966), 97–98.

Pica, Agnoldomenico. *Architettura moderna in Milano: Guida*. Milan, 1964.

In Architectural Review, 135 (May, 1964), 317. Translated in *Boletín Bibliográfico, Instituto interuniversitario de especialización en historia de la arquitectura* (Córdoba, Argentina), no. 8 (Dec., 1965), 53.

Plagemann, Volker. *Das deutsche Kunstmuseum, 1790–1870*. Munich, 1967. (Forschungsunternehmen der Fritz Thyssen Stiftung. Arbeitskreis Kunstgeschichte. Studien zur Kunst des neunzehnten Jahrhunderts, Bd. 3.)

In Burlington Magazine, 110 (Oct., 1968), 584–85.

Plantenga, J. H. *De Akademie van 's Gravenhage en haar Plaats in de Kunst van ons Land*. The Hague, 1937.

In Burlington Magazine, 73 (Aug., 1938), 92.

Pope-Hennessy, James. *History under Fire*. London, 1941. 52 photographs of air-raid damage to London buildings, 1940–41, by Cecil Beaton.

In Burlington Magazine, 79 (Sept., 1941), 101–2.

Posse, Hans. *Der römische Maler Andrea Sacchi*. Leipzig, 1925. (Italienische Forschungen, N.F., Bd. 1.)

In Cronache d'arte, 3 (Jan.–Feb., 1926), 54.

——, ed. *Die Staatliche Gemäldegalerie zu Dresden*. Dresden, 1928.

In Dresdner Anzeiger, Jan. 7, 1929. ("Der grosse Dresdner Galeriekatalog.")

Praz, Mario. *A History of Interior Decoration from Pompeii to Art Nouveau*. [*La filosofia dell'arredamento*.] London, 1965.

In Architectural Review, 138 (July, 1965), 9–12. Illus.

Pühringer, Rudolf. *Denkmäler der früh- und hochromanischen Baukunst in Österreich*. Vienna and Leipzig, 1931. (Denkschriften der Philos.-Hist. Klasse der Akademie der Wissenschaften in Wien, Bd. 70, Abh. 1.)

In Göttingische gelehrte Anzeigen, 195 (April–May, 1933), 178–84.

Rationelle Bebauungsweisen. Frankfurt, 1931. Ergebnisse des 3. Internationalen Kongresses für neues Bauen (Brussels, 1930).

    In Zeitschrift für Ästhetik und Allgemeine Kunstwissenschaft, 27 (1933), 86–89.

Rave, R., and H. J. Knöfel. *Bauen seit 1900 in Berlin.* Berlin, 1968.

    In Architectural Review, 145 (May, 1969), 388.

Reitlinger, Gerald. *The Economics of Taste: The Rise and Fall of Prices, 1760–1960.* London, 1961.

    In Times Literary Supplement, Dec. 8, 1961, p. 880.

Révész-Alexander, Magda. *Die alten Lagerhäuser Amsterdams: eine kunstgeschichtliche Studie.* The Hague, 1928.

    In Deutsche Literaturzeitung, Sept. 13, 1931, col. 1756–59.

Rheims, Maurice. *Art on the Market* [*La vie étrange des objets*]. Tr. by David Pryce-Jones. London, 1961.

    In Times Literary Supplement, Dec. 15, 1961, p. 892.

Richards, James M. *An Introduction to Modern Architecture.* Harmondsworth, 1940.

    In Burlington Magazine, 80 (Jan., 1942), 26.

Rigone, Erice. *L'architetto Andrea Moroni.* Padua, 1939.

    In Burlington Magazine, 76 (Jan., 1940), 34.

Rosenau, Helen. *The Ideal City in Its Architectural Evolution.* London, 1959.

    In Architectural Review, 126 (Oct., 1959), 145.

Rovere, L., V. Viale, and A. E. Brinckmann. *Filippo Juvarra.* Vol. 1. Milan, 1937.

    In Burlington Magazine, 73 (Nov., 1938), 230.

Royal Commission on Historical Monuments. *An Inventory of the Historical Monuments in the City of Cambridge.* London, 1959.

    In Architectural Review, 127 (June, 1960), 369.

Royal Institute of British Architects. *Banister Fletcher Library Drawings Collection: Catalogue of the Drawings of Inigo Jones, John Webb, and Richard Boyle, Third Earl of Burlington, in the Burlington-Devonshire Collection.* London, 1960. Compiled by Prunella Fraser and John Harris.

    In Architectural Review, 129 (May, 1961), 299.

Russell, John (intro.). *State Museums of Berlin.* London, 1964.

    In Times Literary Supplement, Dec. 10, 1964, p. 1120.

Samuel, Enid Cecil. *Villas in Regents Park and Their Residents.* London, 1959. (St. Marylebone Society Publication, n.s., no. 1.)

In Architectural Review, 127 (April, 1960), 227.

Saxl, F. *English Sculptures of the Twelfth Century*. London, 1954.

In Times Literary Supplement, July 8, 1955, p. 378.

Schapiro, Meyer. *Vincent van Gogh, 1853–1890*. London, 1951. (Library of Great Painters.)

In Spectator, Nov. 16, 1951, p. 660.

Schmutzler, Robert. *Jugendstil*. Stuttgart, 1963.

In Architectural Review, 134 (Sept., 1963), 154. Translated in *Boletín Bibliográfico, Instituto interuniversitario de especialización en historia de la arquitectura* (Córdoba, Argentina), no. 6 (Dec., 1964), 33.

Sedlmayr, Hans. *Die Entstehung der Kathedrale*. Zurich, 1950.

In Times Literary Supplement, Jan. 4, 1952, p. 10.

Sekler, Eduard F. *Wren and His Place in European Architecture*. London, 1956.

In Times Literary Supplement, June 15, 1956, pp. 353–54.

Semper, Gottfried. *Wissenschaft, Industrie und Kunst*. Mainz and Berlin, 1968. (Neue Bauhausbücher, Neue Folge.)

In Architectural Review, 145 (March, 1969), 228.

Sharp, Dennis. *Modern Architecture and Expressionism*. London, 1966.

In Architectural Review, 141 (June, 1967), 407.

[Short book reviews.]

In Listener, Jan. 11, 1962, pp. 81–82. ("The Topography of England.")

Simpson, William Douglas. *The Castle at Bergen and the Bishop's Palace at Kirkwall*. Edinburgh, London, 1961. (Aberdeen University Studies, no. 142.)

In Architectural Review, 130 (Dec., 1961), 375.

Sitte, Camillo. *The Art of Building Cities*. Tr. by Charles T. Stewart. New York, 1945.

In Architectural Review, 100 (Dec., 1946), 186.

Sponsel, Jean Louis. *Der Zwinger, die Hoffeste, und die Schlossbaupläne zu Dresden*. Dresden, 1924.

In Belvedere, 13 (July, 1928), 21–23.

Stoddard, Whitney S. *The West Portals of Saint-Denis and Chartres: Sculpture in the Ile de France from 1140 to 1190: Theory of Origins*. Cambridge, Mass., 1952.

In Times Literary Supplement, Jan. 16, 1953, p. 38.

Stonorov. O., and W. Boesiger, eds. and trs. *Le Corbusier und Jeanneret: Ihr gesamtes Werk von 1910 bis 1929.* Zurich, 1930.

In GÖTTINGISCHE GELEHRTE ANZEIGEN, 193 (Aug., 1931), 303–12.

Stroud, Dorothy. *The Architecture of Sir John Soane.* London, 1961.

In MANCHESTER GUARDIAN, Dec. 20, 1961. ("The Lonely Genius of Sir John Soane.")

——. *Capability Brown.* London, 1950.

In CAMBRIDGE REVIEW, 72 (April 21, 1951), 432–34.

Studies in Western Art: Acts of the 20th International Congress of the History of Art. Princeton, 1963.

In TIMES LITERARY SUPPLEMENT, Aug. 20, 1964, p. 740.

Summerson, Sir John. *The Architectural Association, 1847–1947.* London, 1947.

In ARCHITECTURAL REVIEW, 104 (March, 1948), 121.

——. *Georgian London.* London, 1945.

In BURLINGTON MAGAZINE, 88 (May, 1946), 129–30.

——, ed. *The Book of Architecture of John Thorpe in Sir John Soane's Museum.* London, 1964–66. (Walpole Society, vol. 40.)

In ARCHITECTURAL REVIEW, 140 (Dec., 1966), 399–400. ("Summerson on Thorpe.")

Sweeney, James Johnson, and Josep Lluís Sert. *Antoni Gaudí.* London, 1960.

In ARCHITECTS' JOURNAL, Dec. 15, 1960, p. 852.

Symonds, Robert W. *Masterpieces of English Furniture and Clocks.* London, 1940.

In SPECTATOR, Nov. 22, 1940, p. 552.

Taut, Bruno. *Frühlicht.* Ed. by Ulrich Conrads. Frankfurt, Vienna, 1962. (Ullstein Bauwelt-Fundamente.)

In ARCHITECTURAL REVIEW, 136 (Nov., 1964), 319. Illus.

Tedeschi, Enrico. *L'architettura in Inghilterra.* Florence, 1944.

In ARCHITECTURAL REVIEW, 105 (Feb., 1949), 96.

Tessin, Nicodème. *Les relations artistiques entre la France et la Suède, 1693–1718: Nicodème Tessin le jeune et Daniel Cronström, Correspondance: Extraits.* Stockholm, 1964. (Nationalmusei Skriftserie.)

In TIMES LITERARY SUPPLEMENT, Dec. 10, 1964, p. 1120.

Thompson, Paul. *The Work of William Morris.* London, 1967.

In ARCHITECTURAL REVIEW, 144 (Oct., 1968), 287–88. ("Triple Morris.")

Tolnay, Charles de. *Michelangelo*. Vol. 1. *The Youth of Michelangelo*. Princeton, London, 1943.

In TIMES LITERARY SUPPLEMENT, Nov. 8, 1947, p. 578.

———. *Michelangelo*. Vol. 2. *The Sistine Ceiling*. Princeton, London, 1945.

In TIMES LITERARY SUPPLEMENT, March 15, 1947, pp. 109–10.

———. *Michelangelo*. Vol. 5. *The Final Period*. Princeton, London, 1960.

In TIMES LITERARY SUPPLEMENT, Jan. 27, 1961, p. 49.

Tomrley, C. G. *Furnishing Your Home*. London, 1940.

In ARCHITECTURAL REVIEW, 88 (Nov., 1940), 153–54.

Toynbee, Jocelyn, and John Ward Perkins. *The Shrine of St. Peter and the Vatican Excavations*. London, 1956.

In TIMES LITERARY SUPPLEMENT, Feb. 8, 1957, p. 83.

Trincanato, Egle Renata. *Venezia minore*. Milan, 1948.

In ARCHITECTURAL REVIEW, 107 (May, 1950), 351–53. Illus. Plans.

Tubbs, Ralph. *The Englishman Builds*. Harmondsworth, 1945.

In BURLINGTON MAGAZINE, 88 (Dec., 1946), 318.

University of Pennsylvania Bicentennial Conference. *Studies in the Arts and Architecture*. Philadelphia, 1941.

In BURLINGTON MAGAZINE, 86 (April, 1945), 103.

Vale, Edward. *Ancient England: A Review of Monuments and Remains in Public Care and Ownership*. London and Malvern Wells, 1941.

In ARCHITECTURAL REVIEW, 90 (Dec., 1941), 182. [Signed by Peter F. R. Donner, i.e., Nikolaus Pevsner.]

Van de Velde, Henry. *Geschichte meines Lebens*. Munich, 1962.

In TIMES LITERARY SUPPLEMENT, Dec. 28, 1962, p. 1006.

Venditti, Arnaldo. *Architettura neoclassica a Napoli*. Naples, 1961.

In ARCHITECTURAL REVIEW, 131 (May, 1962), 307.

Veronesi, Giulia, and J. Hoffmann, eds. *Josef Hoffmann*. Milan, 1956. (Architetti del movimento moderno, 17.)

In ARCHITECTURAL REVIEW, 123 (May, 1958), 347.

Voss, Hermann. *Die Malerei des Barock in Rom*. Berlin, 1924.

In KUNSTWANDERER, 7 (Nov., 1925).

Wall, V. I. van de. *Het hollandsche koloniale barokmeubel*. Antwerp, The Hague, 1939.

In BURLINGTON MAGAZINE, 76 (June, 1940), 202–3.

Warburg, Aby. *Gesammelte Schriften*. Bd. 1, 2: *Die Erneuerung der heidnischen Antike. Kulturwissenschaftliche Beiträge zur Geschichte der europäischen Renaissance: Mit einem Anhang unveröffentlichter Zusätze.* Ed. by Gertrud Bing. Leipzig, 1932. (Veröffentlichungen der Bibliothek Warburg, Bd. 142.)

> In Theologische Literaturzeitung, 58 (Dec. 23, 1933), col. 465–70.

Watkinson, Roy. *William Morris as Designer.* London, 1967.

> In Architectural Review, 144 (Oct., 1968), 287–88. ("Triple Morris.")

Watts, Stephen. *The Ritz.* London, 1963.

> In Architectural Review, 136 (July, 1964), 7.

Webb, Geoffrey. *Baroque Art.* London, 1949.

> In Architectural Review, 107 (May, 1950), 354.

Webb, Marjorie. *Michael Rysbrack, Sculptor.* London, 1954.

> In Architectural Review, 118 (Oct., 1955), 260.

Weingartner, Josef. *Der Geist des Barock.* Augsburg, 1925.

> In Zeitschrift für bildende Kunst, 61, "Kunstchronik," Nov., 1927, p. 88.

Weisbach, Werner. *Der Barock als Kunst der Gegenreformation.* Berlin, 1921.

> In Repertorium für Kunstwissenschaft, 46 (1925), 243–62.

———. *Spanish Baroque Art: Three Lectures.* Cambridge, 1941.

> In Burlington Magazine, 81 (July, 1942), 208.

Whinney, Margaret, and Oliver Millar. *English Art, 1625–1714.* Oxford, 1957. (Oxford History of English Art, vol. 8.)

> In Architectural Review, 123 (March, 1958), 209–10.

White, James F. *The Cambridge Movement: The Ecclesiologists and the Gothic Revival.* Cambridge, 1962.

> In Times Literary Supplement, Feb. 22, 1963, pp. 124–25.

Wingler, Hans M. *Das Bauhaus, 1919–1933: Weimar, Dessau, Berlin.* Bramsche, 1962.

> In Listener, Jan. 24, 1963, pp. 160–61. Illus. ("Any Old Bauhaus?")

Winstone, Reece. *Bristol, 1950–53.* Bristol, 1965.

> In Architectural Review, 137 (Feb., 1965), 99.

Wölfflin, Heinrich. *Gedanken zur Kunstggeschichte.* 4th ed. Basel, 1947.

> In Burlington Magazine, 89 (Sept., 1947), 260–62.

———. *Kleine Schriften.* Ed. by J. Gantner. Basel, 1946.

> In Burlington Magazine, 89 (Sept., 1947), 260–62.

——. *Renaissance and Baroque.* Tr. by Kathrin Simon. London, 1964.

In Times Literary Supplement, June 25, 1964, p. 544.

Wood, Margaret E. *The English Mediaeval House.* London, 1965.

In Architectural Review, 139 (March, 1966), 173.

Works of Art in Italy: Losses and Survivals in the War. Pt. 2. H.M.S.O.: London, 1946.

In Architectural Review, 102 (Aug., 1947), 68.

Wright, Frank Lloyd. *An Autobiography.* London, 1945.

In Burlington Magazine, 89 (June, 1947), 169.

——. *An Organic Architecture, the Architecture of Democracy: The Sir George Watson Lectures for 1939.* London, 1939.

In Architectural Review, 90 (Aug., 1941), 68–70. [Signed by Peter F. R. Donner, i.e., Nikolaus Pevsner.]

Wüsten, Ernst. *Die Architektur des Manierismus in England.* Leipzig, 1951.

In Architectural Review, 113 (Feb., 1953), 123–24.

Zádor, Anna. *Pollack Mihaly.* Budapest, 1960.

In Architectural Review, 128 (Nov., 1960), 323.

Zarnecki, George. *English Romanesque Sculpture, 1066–1140.* London 1951.

In Architectural Review, 112 (July, 1952), 54.

——. *Later English Romanesque Sculpture, 1140–1210.* London, 1953.

In Architectural Review, 115 (May, 1954), 346.

——. *Polish Art.* Birkenhead, 1945.

In Architectural Review, 98 (Nov., 1945), 148. [Signed by Peter F. R. Donner, i.e., Nikolaus Pevsner.]

Zürcher, Richard. *Der Anteil der Nachbarländer an der Entwicklung der deutschen Baukunst im Zeitalter des Spätbarocks.* Basel, 1938. (Ars docta.)

In Burlington Magazine, 89 (March, 1947), 81–82.

Writings About Sir Nikolaus Pevsner

Banham, Reyner. "Pelican World History of Art in Forty-Eight Volumes," *Architectural Review,* 114 (Nov., 1953), 285–88.

Labò, Mario. "Prefazione," *in* N. B. L. Pevsner. *Storia dell'architettura europea.* Bari, 1959. pp. [vii]–xi.

"Chronicler of Britain." *Observer,* March 31, 1959. The *Observer* profile.

MacInnes, Colin. "The Englishness of Dr. Pevsner," *Twentieth Century,* Jan., 1960, pp. 20–28.

    Reprinted in *England, Half English: A Polyphoto of the Fifties.* Harmondsworth: Penguin Books, 1961. pp. 121–30.

Bohigas, Oriol. "Pròleg a l'edició catalana [of *Outline of European Architecture*]," *in* N. B. L. Pevsner. *Iniciació a l'arquitectura.* Barcelona, 1962, pp. 5–9.

"The Royal Gold Medal: Nikolaus Pevsner," *Journal of the Royal Institute of British Architects,* 3rd ser., 74 (Jan., 1967), 9–10. Portrait. [Signed P. F. R .D.] Translated in *Boletín Bibliográfico, Instituto interuniversitario de especialización en historia de la arquitectura* (Córdoba, Argentina), no. 9 (Dec., 1967), 5.

"Dr. Pevsner Gets R.I.B.A. Award as Writer: Scholar with Passion for Buildings," *Times,* Jan. 4, 1967.

"Royal Gold for Pevsner," *Architects' Journal,* Jan. 4, 1967, pp. 71–72.

"Royal Gold Medallist," *Building,* Jan. 6, 1967, p. 50.

"A Jolly Good Fellow," *Architects' Journal*, April, 1967, pp. 209–10. ("Astragal.")

Hughes-Stanton, Corin. "Nikolaus Pevsner: A Major Influence on Modern Design," *Design*, June, 1967, pp. 56–57. Portrait.

"Dr. Pevsner Royal Gold Medallist," *Financial Times*, June 20, 1967.

"Royal Gold Medal Award: Sir John Summerson's Tribute to Nikolaus Pevsner [June 20, 1967.]," *Architects' Journal*, June 28, 1967, pp. 1523–24.

"Honouring Nikolaus Pevsner. Royal Gold Medal Night at the RIBA," *Building*, June 30, 1967, p. 78.

"Gold Medallist, 1967," *Architectural Review*, 142 (Aug., 1967), 79–80. An anthology of tributes that appeared in the press.

Summerson, Sir John, and R. Sheppard. "Nikolaus Pevsner, 1967 Gold Medallist," *Journal of the Royal Institute of British Architects*, 3rd ser., 74 (Aug., 1967), 316–18.

"Homenaje à Pevsner," *Boletín Bibliografico, Instituto interuniversitario de especialización en historia de la arquitectura* (Córdoba, Argentina), no. 9 (Dec., 1967), 5.

Summerson, Sir John, ed. *Concerning Architecture: Essays on Architectural Writers and Writing Presented to Nikolaus Pevsner*. London: Allen Lane, The Penguin Press, 1968. xii. 316 pp. Illus. Bibliog.

> REVIEW:
>
> *Times Literary Supplement*, May 15, 1969. Letter from Sir Nikolaus Pevsner, *ibid.*, May 29, p. 584 in answer to review.

R., J. "Sir Nikolaus Pevsner (1000 Makers of the Twentieth Century)," *Sunday Times*, Aug. 24, 1969, color suppl.

Index